Praise for

What a privilege it is to endorse *Undefiled Access*. Elizabeth has done an incredible job and written such an amazing book that personally I found to be insightful, thought provoking, encouraging, refreshing, and continually pointing to the beauty of Jesus. As a minister of healing for over 20 years and having a daughter with disabilities, this is a book that will bless many people into understanding the journey of disabilities, which is often is so misunderstood. Greater than this though, she reveals the heart of the heavenly Father on every page. Thank you, Elizabeth, for writing such a profound book. I found myself gripped on reading the manuscript and really look forward to getting a paper copy and taking the time to dive deeper into every word on each page. I encourage others to do so also.

—Chris Gore
Author, *Apprehended Identity and Walking in Supernatural Healing Power*; Chris Gore Ministries

Profound. Compassionate. Raw. Real. Challenging. Brilliant. These words describe, but do not adequately capture the essence of Elizabeth's book that is so infused with her own indefatigable spirit. As her pastors, we know her to be an amazing woman of God, filled with the Holy Spirit, and well-equipped to write this groundbreaking book.

—Happy and Dianne Leman
Founding Pastors, The Vineyard Church of Central IL, Urbana, IL

Elizabeth Flora-Swick's wonderful book *Undefiled Access*, is a prophetic call to the Charismatic/Pentecostal movements. It's an honest appeal to Christians who truly believe in the present-day healing ministry of Jesus, yet find the presence of people with disabilities uncomfortable due to our inability to live with the mysteries of God in the church. Elizabeth's story and perspective as one who had experienced being treated as a "second class citizen" (her words) by Spirit-filled believers is heartbreakingly transparent and real.

However, she leads us in love to a place where we will love and treat people with disabilities as powerful brothers and sisters. She gives helpful advice on how to relate to these dear believers and raise them up to a place of honor and deep respect for the treasures that they are. I highly recommend this book to any church leader who has a desire for the church to be a culture of honor for all sons and daughters of God, as well as to those in the healing ministry who will love the disability community as they are. Thank you, Elizabeth, for this powerful work!

—**Dr. Mike Hutchings**
Director, Global Awakening School of Ministry,
Mechanicsburg, PA; President, God Heals PTSD Foundation;
Author, *Supernatural Freedom from the Captivity of Trauma*

Elizabeth's compelling book encourages believers to be intentional and diligent about cultivating intimacy with God. In part of her book, she specifically addresses some of the challenges that believers with disabilities face growing in deeper intimacy with the living God. She speaks from years of personal experience in this. As she is boldly believing God to heal her body, she continues to grow in her enjoyment of God's presence in her life. Our access by the Holy Spirit to the Father is both the catalyst for an effective supernatural lifestyle and a refuge in the storm of circumstances. From this place, Elizabeth showcases the freedom to celebrate Jesus's beauty as we wait in hope for all of God's promises.

—**Mike Bickle**
International House of Prayer
of Kansas City

I am so deeply grateful for Elizabeth for writing *Undefiled Access*! In these pages, you'll find a treasure trove of wisdom, authenticity, vulnerability, truth, and a precious window into what it looks like to live as a passionate pursuer of the Spirit-filled life while a member of the disability community. Elizabeth wrestles with tensions as deep as they come as she exhorts us to live fully faithful to the gospel of Jesus the miracle worker, while also truly loving each disabled person in a way that acknowledges their reality and refuses to settle for shallow or dishonoring "easy answers." Reading this book opened my eyes in powerful ways and made me a better practitioner of the ministry of the kingdom. I'm so glad to have read it, and I recommend it to you as well!

—**Putty Putman**
Author, *Live Like Jesus* and *Kingdom Impact*

UNDEFILED ACCESS

Healing the Worldview Divide between
Charismatic Christianity
and the Disability Community

ELIZABETH FLORA-SWICK

Undefiled Access
Copyright © 2023 Elizabeth Flora-Swick
Urbana, IL | www.elizabethfloraswick.com

All rights reserved. No part of this publication may be reproduced, distributed, or transmitted in any form or by any means, including photocopying, recording, or other electronic or mechanical methods, without the prior written permission of the publisher, except in the case of brief quotations embodied in critical reviews and certain other noncommercial uses permitted by copyright law.

All Scripture quotations, unless otherwise indicated, are taken from the Holy Bible, New International Version®, NIV®. Copyright © 1973, 1978, 1984, 2011 by Biblica, Inc.™ Used by permission of Zondervan. All rights reserved worldwide. www.zondervan.com. The "NIV" and "New International Version" are trademarks registered in the United States Patent and Trademark office by Biblica, Inc.™

Scripture quotations marked (ESV) are from the Holy Bible, English Standard Version® (ESV®), copyright © 2001 by Crossway, a publishing ministry of Good News Publishers. Used by permission. All rights reserved.

Scripture quotations marked (NKJV) are from The Holy Bible, New King James Version®. Copyright © 1982 by Thomas Nelson. Used by permission. All rights reserved.

Scripture quotations marked (NLT) are taken from the *Holy Bible*, New Living Translation, copyright © 1996, 2004, 2015 by Tyndale House Foundation. Used by permission of Tyndale House Publishers, Carol Stream, Illinois 60188. All rights reserved.

Editing by Amber Helt at Rooted in Writing, rootedinwriting.com
Cover design by Jonathan Lewis at Jonlin Creative, jonlincreative.com
Book design by Jody Skinner at Skinner Book Services, skinnerbooks.com

Library of Congress Control Number: 2023900380
ISBN: 979-8-9875864-1-9 (paperback), 979-8-9875864-0-2 (e-book)

DEDICATION

*To the dearest and best in my life, the Holy Spirit.
Thank you for keeping my heart and
faithfully revealing Jesus and the Father.
It is my greatest joy to watch you make Jesus's name
remembered in my generation.*

CONTENTS

Foreword		xi
	Introduction: A Daughter's Perspective	1
1	Access	17
2	Lovesick for the Bleeding Healer	37
3	Little Seed	53
4	Social Construct or Identity? (Disability Culture Part 1)	73
5	The Eugenics Fallout (Disability Culture Part 2)	87
6	The Exodus God	101
7	The Dignity of Three-Dimensional Existence	121
8	Healing According to the Flesh	143
9	A Love Affair with Performance	165
10	Trading Heaven's Glory to Magnify Hell	185
11	Love Makes a Way	203
12	Love Touches Deeply	227
13	Love Restores Majestically	251
Additional Resources		273
Acknowledgments		275
Notes		277

FOREWORD

Undefiled Access has a greater reach than just the Charismatic and disability communities. It will inspire anyone who reads it to anchor your heart deeper into the gospel. It will open the eyes of your understanding that the Father, Son, and Spirit have torn the veil of separation. Through the cross of suffering, a doorway of access has opened, and all are invited to enter into the healing heart of a good God who longs to lavish His love upon us. It's access into communion to hear the voice of the Good Shepherd so we won't wander aimlessly into the shadows of hopelessness and despair or into the entrapment and lure of sin. Rather, we are embraced by the open arms of the Father so we can live in the light of His delight, no matter the suffering we experience.

Elizabeth's book will take you on a journey where you will see faith, hope, and love experienced through her story. The story of healing is also the story of suffering. I love the beautiful imagery of the risen Messiah who still bears the nail-pierced scars on his hands and feet. The resurrection and life-giver of all still bears the marks of His suffering. It's a testimony that he understands our pain and struggles. He is the great high priest who intercedes for us as one who knows pain. He is Emmanuel, God with us, in our darkness and despair. His scars testify that our scars and pain cannot hold us in the grave. We have been given the resurrection life that speaks louder than the trauma we have encountered. The resurrected Messiah has defeated death, hell, and the grave and has set us free despite our struggles.

Elizabeth invites us to an even greater understanding of healing that doesn't limit or deny physical healing but embraces the mystery and tension of the now-but-not-fully yet of the gospel of the kingdom. Though her disability is a reality that she experiences, it doesn't define her. Rather, it refines her into a deeper place of gospel healing that has opened up a realm of access offered to all. Yet, few of us have embraced the depth of this good news as Elizabeth has.

She will help you see through the perspective of someone who faces the challenges of disability, living as a charismatic believer practicing the *charismata* (spiritual gifts) of the Holy Spirit, including the gift of healing. You will also learn how to see those with disabilities more clearly and embrace their gifting and calling now, not just when they are made whole. We need to stop seeing them only as broken people needing to be healed, or worse, as a target for healing practice. Rather, they are fellow believers who have something to contribute, like all who are becoming healed as we embrace the glorious gospel—Jesus.

This book is filled with treasures of the Holy Spirit's whispers all along the way. You will find yourself wanting to dig deeper into these nuggets of wisdom, engage in these Gospel invitations, and access the deep intimacy that Elizabeth has cultivated with the Father, Son, and Spirit.

—Brian Blount
Author, speaker, and pastor
Crestwood Vineyard Church, OKC
Putting Jesus on Display with Love and Power

AUTHOR'S NOTE ON TERMINOLOGY

Throughout this book, I use the terminology *people with disabilities* and *disabled people* interchangeably. While I prefer person-first language (the former term) rather than identity-first language (the latter term), I switch between both descriptors.

I also use the terms *Spirit-filled*, *charismatic*, and *supernatural* Christianity to avoid redundancy in describing Christians who believe continuationist theology. I am not suggesting that Christians who disagree with this theology do not have, or have less of, God's Spirit living in them. The Holy Spirit is a person who indwells our hearts at salvation. He is not a substance or a force.

Rather than using the common title *Christ*, I routinely refer to Jesus as *the Messiah*. *Christ* is the Greek translation for the Hebrew-based word *Messiah*. I prefer *Messiah* for two reasons:

1. I believe Jesus is the fulfillment of the Bible's messianic prophecies, and it is meaningful for me to use language that encompasses this idea. Only through these promises to the nation of Israel am I saved.

2. There is too much confusion in culture over the word *Christ*. With some people promoting a disembodied Christ, or *Christ consciousness*, it is important to specify Jesus the Messiah is a historic, embodied man who lived, died, and was resurrected to fulfill God's promises to Abraham, Israel, and the world.

If any Jewish readers encounter the messianic language, please know I made this choice to remain faithful to my beliefs. It is not an attempt to appropriate your language or manipulate your beliefs.

INTRODUCTION

A Daughter's Perspective

"I would like full restoration," said the softhearted man. "Do you pray like that?"

"Yes," I answered, a smile nudging my lips.

"I thought so," he replied.

My new friend wanted Jesus to reconcile his family, but not a measured reconciliation. He wanted fullness. So in a university building surrounded by students rushing to class, I requested full restoration from the King of Glory for this precious brother.

Rolling to my dorm in my wheelchair, I could not suppress a full-scale grin at our brief, ironic exchange. At first glance, I am the last person most people would expect to believe in God for fullness. Yet my new friend anticipated my yes. Maybe because I offered to pray with him. Us "fullness" Christians were known for such actions.

But I suspected a deeper recognition occurred. He saw me as I was—a daughter willing to tug on the Father's heartstrings for anyone about anything worth asking for, even fullness. I did not know how else to pray. True to my Father's instruction, we could always ask for his fullness on the earth.

I am a daughter of the charismatic church. I have never experienced a moment when I did not know that God is real, speaks today in all languages, and is intimately involved in all of life. Around the time my parents had children, they discovered the available presence and power of the Holy Spirit. In March 1992, they welcomed their son, Micah. In April 1994, they welcomed four daughters: Rachel, Rebekah, Elizabeth, and Hannah. With five kids ages two and under, my parents quickly learned dependence on God. He *had* to be active in the world because they needed him every day. And as God showed up for them, my parents invited their children to enter a personal knowledge of this available God.

I do not remember my moment of first receiving Jesus, but I know Rachel's salvation story.

At a church in Kansas City, Rachel reported to Mom, "I heard Jesus knocking on the door of my heart."

"Oh, what did you do?" Mom asked.

"I let him in," Rachel answered. She was four years old.

Rachel and her husband, Blake, are now raising their children to know the Holy Spirit's voice.

Rachel once shared with her oldest son, "Do you know the best thing about the Holy Spirit, Judah? He shows us Jesus."

Eyes wide in hopeful wonder, three-year-old Judah asked, "Will the Holy Spirit show me Jesus?"

"Yes, he will," Rachel said. "Ask him, and he will show you Jesus."

What a beautiful privilege to share the Holy Spirit's role with the next generation.

Rebekah calls me "the family vault" because I stored key memories of our childhood. I remember hearing our parents' stories of when they received the gift of tongues and when Dad first saw a deliverance from spiritual darkness. He also shared a dream about Jesus coming into his room during the Toronto Blessing. Dad felt the fiery love of God, his heart burning from proximity to Jesus. I would often ask Dad to retell the story of when Jesus came into his room because I wanted to be ready if Jesus ever came into my room. This was, of course, long before I understood my heart could never be "ready" for such a moment.

Our parents read us the stories of missionaries like Gladys Aylward and George Müeller. They trusted God amid severe pressure, and he provided for them. My sisters and I enacted similar scenarios. We played "the orphanage game." We gathered all our stuffed animals and Beanie Babies, gave them food and medicine from empty boxes of Milk Duds (Hannah's idea), and cared for them. In the course of the game, we would run out of food. So, we prayed and asked Jesus for more. Minutes later, we received a call promising food or a delivery of milk and bread on the doorstep. I have such a clear memory of this because I filed it as valuable. I thought there might be a time when we would do this in real life.

BORN INTO ACCESS

These experiences taught me high expectations of God. I expected God to be present and lived each day with the conviction that he could be personally known. By age nine, I knew the Holy Spirit's voice well enough to decide I knew better than he did. But the Good Shepherd persisted in wooing this little lamb into his heart. I found his tenderness irresistible, and my own tenderness responded.

The sleeping bags in my parents' house must have been anointed. Every time I slept in one, I encountered the Father's affection. It felt like the Holy Spirit wrapped around me. The last time I slept in one on a family camping trip, the Lord's presence and conviction settled over me as soon as I curled into it. I knew who it was. My fifteen-year-old heart had opted for internal rebellion at the time. It made a 180-degree turn and barreled into the Father's arms. His kindness overwhelmed me, and I could not resist his presence. I still cannot.

Beyond a love for his presence, I learned to treasure the gifts of the Holy Spirit. I grew up listening to my parents pray in tongues. I knew it was worshiping God and that it would happen to me one day. I learned to honor prophecy—the ability to hear and speak God's heart. I believed healing was, and always is, possible in any circumstance. My faith is inseparable from the values of the charismatic church. I was born into access.

BORN INTO TENSION

I also have never known a day of wholeness in my body. In the first seconds after birth, I lost oxygen long enough to shut down neurological mechanisms that control muscle function. I do not have the muscle–brain connection that allows people to walk and coordinate movement. The condition—cerebral palsy—affects my entire body, and I use a wheelchair. I have a visible disability I cannot hide. I am a continual disability disclosure.

While I am a daughter of the charismatic church, my experiences there have not been wholly positive and, sometimes, have been deeply painful. Disability and the celebration of God's supernatural power integrate seamlessly inside my soul and spirit, but it can be rather jarring on the other side of my skin.

Charismatic Christians tend to reduce people like me to only disfigured, broken bodies. We easily become second-class citizens in the Father's kingdom or, at worst, invisible nonpersons with no dignity considered worthy of protection. I am painting with broad brush strokes here. Many people have loved me well, and I am grateful. But people with disabilities are, albeit often unintentionally, treated as pending miracles with nothing more to offer the community of believers than justification for the strength of other people's faith. So why have I stayed on the charismatic train?

Could I not go elsewhere and avoid the stigma and presumption? No.

If I left the charismatic church, I could avoid the negative ways some people pray for healing, but the reduction of my being to the weakness in my body would remain. The stigma of disability is itself part of the world system, and it is often uncorrected in all faith communities. It is not a new experience for any disabled person to be defined by our diagnoses and limitations. The only lasting antidote I have found to this stigma is personal access to Jesus's face and connection to a community of people who actively choose to see according to the Spirit of God. Without these two elements, the stigma is present no matter where I go.

The charismatic church has unique potential to be a sanctuary for the disability community. We emphasize the earthly access every person can have to God. For us, eternity always starts today. There is no waiting to be close anymore. The riches of the gospel, or good news, are available for God's sons and daughters to enjoy now while we wait for the final fulfillment of his faithful promises. We have undefiled, unrestricted access to the Father in Jesus through the Holy Spirit.

Charismatic theology also offers the best likelihood of finding people who will see deeper than skin. Everyone who believes the Holy Spirit speaks today has the option to ask God how he sees a person and to respond accordingly. Stigma based on externals could be pruned and removed from our gatherings altogether if we listened to the Father's heart for people before we opened our mouths. I stay because we have beautiful theology. Even though our theology does not always translate into its true beauty in practice, Spirit-filled Christianity can be the safest place on earth for the disability community.

But the Spirit-filled church is far from a sanctuary for most disabled people. The majority of Christians with disabilities attend congregations and build disability ministries where there is no emphasis on the supernatural. They reject charismatic Christianity because of fear and negative experiences validating that fear. Outside the church, members of the disability community interpret the charismatic emphasis on healing as a form of religious stigma directed against their value as human beings.

I understand the fear and rejection from disabled Christians and non-Christians alike. I do not live in denial. There is little I have not experienced in the charismatic church. I have faced the worst and the best of it. Yet, I make a different choice than most. Although I am acutely aware of the problems, I refuse to compare the best of the Father's house with the worst of Satan's fodder. There is a difference between homemade bread and manure. The existence of the second does not delegitimize the wholesome, altogether separate goodness of the first.

CLOSING THE GAP

No one has attempted to heal the divide between charismatic Christianity and disability. Joni Eareckson Tada is the name most Christians think of when they hear the words *disability* and *church* in the same sentence. I greatly respect Joni, and the Spirit-filled church would be wise to use her ministry's resources on accessibility. Joni champions the mandate in Luke 14, the Lord's command that we invite people with disabilities into the kingdom of God. I agree we should intentionally invite this group to the banquet, and I see the strategy of heaven in Joni's life and ministry. The difference between our perspectives is I long for everyone to access not only the banquet food of God's kingdom but also its new wine.

When disability ministries minimize the gifts of the Holy Spirit, they limit access to these legitimate elements of the gospel. Like sexuality and disability, the supernatural and disability are taboo. The not-for-you attitude preventing disabled people from learning about either topic produces similar consequences. If we do not explain healthy sexuality, we leave this group vulnerable to abuse. If we do not share biblical supernatural reality, we leave them vulnerable to the enticing of the false supernatural.

I am not offended by disabled Christians who are uninterested in learning about the Holy Spirit or his works on the earth. We can disagree and remain in unity. My heart breaks, however, for people with disabilities who are not saved and yet are fascinated by the supernatural. From the new age movement to the overt occult, I see people everywhere hungry for spiritual reality. But they opt for imitation and counterfeits instead of biblical, naturally supernatural lives. These are the ones I want in the Father's kingdom.

People with disabilities, like everyone, were made for the Holy Spirit to live inside us and to partner with him for Jesus's fame on the earth. We exist for intimacy with and glorification of God. Even if I am not healed in this life, I still equally participate as a daughter in all the good works the Father is doing. I want disabled people to be discipled to share the gospel, pray for healing, prophesy, give words of knowledge, and speak in and interpret the gift of tongues. The Holy Spirit is not limited by the presence of disability. He will use anyone with a submitted heart.

It is time to close the gap between supernatural Christianity and the disability community. I do not see conflict between these two dimensions. I live at their intersection, and they work together faithfully. Opposing the not-for-you attitude against sharing supernatural Christianity with disabled people, I will repeat Peter's famous words. Cleansing from sin and the promise of the Holy Spirit with all his gifts is assuredly *"for you and your children* and for all who are far off—for all whom the Lord our God will call" (Acts 2:39, emphasis added).

A PEOPLE GROUP

A widely used definition of *disability* comes from the Americans with Disabilities Act (ADA). Under the ADA, disability is "a physical or mental impairment that limits one or more major life activity."[1] Applying this generalized definition, the CDC reports that one in four Americans have a disability and broadly divides disability types into the following categories: mobility, cognition, hearing, vision, independent living, and self-care.[2] There can be overlap across these categories. Someone may have both a hearing and a mobility disability, for example, and the degree of limitation will impact a person's need for care. Given the extensive variation between disability type and degree of limitation, we begin to see the complexity of this population and the impossibility of reducing it to a single factor. Government statistics aside, disabled people in the West began to group identify as a means of advancing their social and civic rights. The term *disability community* expresses this collective. Like all communities, this one developed a unique culture.

The charismatic church should approach disabled people in the same sensitive, humble way we approach any intercultural work. Before entering a culture different from ours, we learn the history, customs, and etiquette so we can honorably communicate the gospel without causing harm. Yet, the Spirit-filled church does not attempt such cultural humility toward disabled people. If we want salvation for this group, we must meet them where they are, discern their hearts' longings, and connect them back to the Father—just like Jesus. Only from that place of covenant restoration, can we even begin to effectively speak truth into the traps of the world system, including its interpretation of disability.

I will be addressing problematic practices in charismatic ministry from the lens of how these actions translate across a culture. Before reacting defensively, remember the intercultural frame. This is not about us or about ministry successes defined on our terms. This is about helping people encounter the love of Jesus and the Father so that many can enter the family of God.

TWO AUDIENCES

My primary audience is any Christian who believes God speaks and moves supernaturally today. If you affirm continuationist theology or describe yourself as charismatic, Pentecostal, Third

Wave Evangelical, or some combination of these terms, welcome aboard. I am as you are, your daughter and your sister. I am glad for your company. I love the Spirit-filled church with a fervent, God-bestowed affection. I would rather wash the feet of the Lord's servants than cut hearts. My primary spiritual gift is encouragement. I prefer to see the best in people, and I have done my best to come as low as possible so my words may strengthen you.

Chapters 8–10, though, are written to cut. Not to cut hearts, but to remove the malignant tumors of religious performance and magnification of the devil from our healing ministries. Yet even in the cutting, this is not an angry tirade. I love you. I am not offended by you. I do not consider myself better than you. If the world up-ended tomorrow, you would find me working shoulder-to-shoulder alongside you so that the glory of Jesus's name would yet be exalted. I simply want us to be healthy. I want us to grow together into all Jesus calls us to become in this hour.

Because you are my primary audience, you will have the best context for the content. I expect you to have a baseline understanding of hearing God's voice and the gifts of the Holy Spirit. I will not be detailing these concepts (e.g., differences between a prophetic word and a word of knowledge). There are other books available. Outside a few statements below and a limited overview of biblical texts in chapter 2, do not anticipate arguments for God's supernatural activity through his people today. For me, these truths are self-apparent from the Scripture, and this book is not the vehicle for their lengthy discussion.

But yes, God moves in power and speaks today. My favorite,

and perhaps the most underrated, biblical evidence for the Holy Spirit's voice to his people is found in 3 John. John writes to his friend Gaius about a man named Demetrius in these words: "Demetrius is well spoken of by everyone—and even by the truth itself. We also speak well of him, and you know that our testimony is true" (3 John 12).

"The truth itself" speaks well of Demetrius—The Spirit of Truth.[3] We should make it the aim of our lives for "the truth" to also speak well of us. There is an abundance of texts confirming God speaks to his people,[4] but I cannot share them here.

My final comment on the Holy Spirit's activity is a recommendation to take a global perspective. Only in the Western church is there a debate on whether God speaks and moves supernaturally. In the global church, it is not questioned. Nearly every Christian is "charismatic" outside the West, and even more so where there is persecution for one's faith. These brothers and sisters are depending on the Spirit of God, and the good news is when we need him, he is there. The difference between the Western and global church is our hearts often have not been as deeply pierced by the truth of how dependent we are on the Holy Spirit.

I mention the difference between the Western and global church because this book is directed toward the church in the West. I've minimally traveled outside the United States, and the bulk of my experience is connected to Christianity in a Western frame. I also do not know what it is like to experience disability outside the West.

To the Disability Community

If you consider yourself to be a member of the disability community, Christian or non-Christian, welcome aboard also. You are my honored guests. Although most of these pages are written for the church, I wrote the first three chapters with you in my heart. I attempted to communicate the riches I found in the gospel of Jesus. I added details of my relationship with God I never expected to share publicly because he asked me to showcase how access works in his kingdom. You deserve to know how much Jesus has done for me.

I did not write these details so churchgoers could flatter me. I did not write them to raise myself above you. I wrote them hoping they are specific enough to stir your heart to jealousy for the abundant delight I enjoy in my God. I only shared a few drops of the ocean of goodness available in the Father's house. The door, of course, is wide open for you to experience the same satisfaction. Come with me and taste for yourselves that the Lord is good.

Although I have a disability, I am different from many of you. Chapters 4–6 will likely cause friction for my disabled guests. I disagree with the worldview claim that disability is ontological—a big, philosophical word for "connected to one's being." Disability is no one's identity.

I do not find the disability identity worldview anywhere in Scripture, and the arguments claiming to substantiate it are anchored in humanism rather than biblical truth. Nor does the identity concept hold its weight in the honest evaluation of our lives. If you must label me an *ableist* for these beliefs, I respect your freedom to do so. I only ask that you try listening to me as I have listened to you over many years.

My separation of disability and identity is not because I am afflicted by internalized judgment against my own body. My worldview runs oppositely. I consider my body of such great worth that the Messiah died to restore it—more than that, to give me a new, eternal, glorified one eventually. Jesus paid highly for the reconciliation of all creation. He is in charge of whether I experience a measure of that reconciliation prior to a new heaven and earth. But in either case, disability is set to expire. So it cannot be affixed to my being.

But I won't try to convince you of God's healing power as a prerequisite for acceptance. God's heart is more generous than that, and so is mine. I recognize the costliness of living into Christian supernatural reality in a world that would prefer you do not exist.

I am grateful you exist. You are made for daily, heart-to-heart intimacy with your Creator. God wants you. Before you write off supernatural Christianity, it is only fair to give the triune God a chance to communicate and demonstrate his affection. He is in pursuit of you now, as you are. He knows you intricately already and loves what he knows. Tender, isn't it?

MAJESTICALLY GOOD

I request neither audience read chapters 8–10 without chapters 11–13. I explained negative practices in Spirit-filled spaces to demonstrate the truth and beauty of the alternatives. Jesus—and the Father he represents through the Holy Spirit—is altogether lovely. I have never met anyone who treated me with more respect and kindness than the triune God. His misrepresentation by the mistakes of his people, myself included, does not diminish the goodness of who God is and what his heart is truly like.

I had every chance to close my heart in bitterness from the pain I experienced in the church. I had every human-centered reason to deconstruct my faith if I based my response to God upon how people in the church responded to me. But that choice betrays a false logic. Since when did the uncreated God become the mistakes of his image bearers?

In the summer of 2021, I sat in the back row of church, my heart consumed in crafting this book. Its completion required me to traverse the minefields of misunderstanding that characterize a disabled charismatic's territory—a no-man's-land caught in frenetic worldview crossfire. The clamoring frustration in my soul accurately signaled the difficulty of the task ahead.

At the end of the message, a teenager came on stage to prophesy. His piercing exhortation from Revelation 1 joined immediately with the Holy Spirit's internal witness. The young man called us to fascinate our hearts with Jesus—the resurrected, glorious Messiah whose eyes blaze with holy fire. The thought—*This is why I am charismatic*—instantly ordered my internal chaos.

I want to be with people who call my gaze back to Jesus's beauty, majesty, and worth. I was that teenager fascinated by the God-man with eyes of fire. The Holy Spirit and I remain in sweet agreement that Jesus is matchless. He sits far above every other authority. His power is sufficient to heal the nations and restore creation now and forever. Any presentation of another Jesus remains hollow. Any path that does not lead us to his beautiful, resurrected face is not worth the walking.

Instead of retracting my heart in offense, I have offered it, wounds and all, to the King of Glory. God is worthy of this offering. He is far better and more beautiful than most people have ever considered.

Here is an overview of what to expect in the rest of these pages. My readers will:

- Enjoy a fresh invitation to the intimate access we have to God in Jesus.
- Discover how the gospel answers the worldview questions of disability culture.
- Correct harmful healing ministry practices to reconnect love with power in charismatic spaces.
- Gain theological and practical tools to minister naturally and supernaturally to people with disabilities.

CHAPTER 1

Access

I'll make this as clear as the glassy sea. There are some promises for which I am willing to wait—access to God is not one of them. Imagine living in a world where most of the physical and social infrastructure was built as if you do not exist. That *is* the world for people with disabilities. To us, access is everything. Access extends acceptance; barriers communicate rejection. If there is one presentation of the gospel that will move the hearts of the disability community to Jesus, it begins with access.

I can count on one hand the number of accessible houses I have entered. Almost all homes are built with stairs. The ratio of truly accessible doors is on a similar scale. The tangible discovery that the Father's house is permanently open and available to me at all times without restriction is akin to waking up one morning to the phone call that I've inherited Bezos's and Gates's fortunes combined. Yet even this analogy breaks down in the end. The sum treasure of all the world could never equalize the balance of value in the gospel of the Messiah.

THE NARRATIVE AND ITS CLIMAX

When God created the world, he gave humanity perfect access to himself. He made human beings in his image to live in holy relationship with God and one another. At the moment of sin, humanity lost their access to God and their relationship with each other fractured.

The Bible's plot revolves around how God reverses this situation, providing a way for people to have undefiled access to himself and one another again. From God's covenant with Abraham through the exodus of Israel from Egypt and beyond, the plot moves toward resolving this conflict. As it moves, the tension grows. Israel has God's presence with them in the tabernacle and the temple, but they are exiled from their land, and the Babylonians destroy the temple. When a remnant of Israel returns, they rebuild the Jerusalem temple and wait for the promised Messiah Moses and the prophets said would come to rescue them. As Jeremiah prophesied,

> "This is the covenant I will make with the people of Israel
>   after that time," declares the LORD.
> "I will put my law in their minds
>   and write it on their hearts.

> I will be their God,
>> and they will be my people.
> No longer will they teach their neighbor,
>> or say to one another, 'Know the Lord,'
> because they will all know me,
>> from the least of them to the greatest,"
>> declares the Lord.
> "For I will forgive their wickedness
>> and will remember their sins no more."
>> (Jer. 31:33–34)

God's deliverance from sin and the restoration of access to himself came through Israel's Messiah, Jesus, and extends to all people on earth. In this way, God fulfilled his promise to Abraham that "all peoples on earth will be blessed through you" (Gen. 12:3). Or in Isaiah's language:

> In the last days
> the mountain of the Lord's temple will be established
>> as the highest of the mountains;
> it will be exalted above the hills,
>> and all nations will stream to it.
>> (Isa. 2:2)

The climax of the Bible's conflict is not the Messiah's resurrection, though. His resurrection initiates the plot resolution. The climax is a ripped cloth. Mark's gospel tells us: "With a loud cry, Jesus breathed his last. The curtain of the temple was torn in two from top to bottom" (Mark 15:37–38).

The curtain in the Jerusalem temple split in top-down fashion as Jesus took his final breath on the cross. The significance of this torn fabric was that for the first time since sin, we gained permanent access to God again. The writer of the book of Hebrews details our access:

> Therefore, brothers and sisters, since we have confidence to enter the Most Holy Place by the blood of Jesus, by a new and living way opened for us through the curtain, that is, his body, and since we have a great priest over the house of God, let us draw near to God with a sincere heart and with the full assurance that faith brings, having our hearts sprinkled to cleanse us from a guilty conscience and having our bodies washed with pure water. Let us hold unswervingly to the hope we profess, for he who promised is faithful. (Heb. 10:19–23)

He who promised is indeed faithful. The way to the Father is open. I will hold unswervingly to this hope and humbly enter God's presence. None of us produced this access. God accomplished it on his own for all of us, which Paul reminds us in his letter to the Ephesians:

> But because of his great love for us, God, who is rich in mercy, made us alive with Christ even when

we were dead in transgressions—it is by grace you have been saved. And God raised us up with Christ and seated us with him in the heavenly realms in Christ Jesus, in order that in the coming ages he might show the incomparable riches of his grace, expressed in his kindness to us in Christ Jesus. (Eph. 2:4–7)

Not only are we saved from sin; we are also made alive with the Messiah. Jesus did not stay dead, and neither do we. He lives forever, and we are granted entry through this magnificent High Priest to worship and serve the Father all our days. It is from this purchased, secure position that we can approach God in full assurance.

BIDIRECTIONAL ACCESS

There is another layer to the goodness of this accessible gospel. In Jesus, we have perfect access to God, but wonder of wonders, God has perfect access to us. We have the Holy Spirit inside us.

Ponder again the torn temple veil. The temple represented the throne of God in heaven and was a tangible space where God's presence intersected with the earth. Through his death and resurrection, Jesus established a new kind of temple. Corporately and individually, Christians become the temple of God, the new intersecting point between God's presence and the earth.

Paul communicates the corporate aspect when he writes to the Corinthians, "Don't you know that you yourselves are God's temple and that God's Spirit dwells in your midst?" (1 Cor. 3:16). Later in the same letter, Paul explains we are also individual temples who carry God's presence in our physical bodies. Paul reinforces, "Do you not know that your bodies are temples of the Holy Spirit, who is in you, whom you have received from God? You are not your own" (1 Cor. 6:19).

Peter likewise beautifully interweaves this bidirectional access when he reminds persecuted Christians,

> As you come to him, the living Stone—rejected by humans but chosen by God and precious to him— you also, like living stones, are being built into a spiritual house to be a holy priesthood, offering spiritual sacrifices acceptable to God through Jesus Christ. (1 Pet. 2:4–5)

Corporately, we are stones forming God's temple and priests with unqualified access to God. Individually, our lives function like the holy of holies in the temple. We house the Holy Spirit. This does not mean we become God. It means God's Spirit lives in our hearts. We are the house, and we remain the house. As he lives in us, the Holy Spirit reinstates our capacity to live as human beings who reflect the image of God.[5] The triune God reconnects the original relational ties set at the world's beginning.

Some Christians treat access to God like a someday reality with an emphasis on waiting for it when we die or when Jesus returns. While there is truth to that perspective, it is incomplete.

The full restoration of heaven and earth has not happened, and we do not yet experience the blissful perfection of God's glory covering the whole earth.[6] While on this earth, we live by faith because we are not physically with the Lord.[7]

Our access to God, though, is set. I cannot physically see God when I spend time with him. But I do not need to see him to love him[8] or to know we are close. I can dwell in the house of the Lord forever.[9] Forever includes today.

Consider strings on a weaving loom. While our relationships with God will no doubt deepen in richness and texture across the tapestry of eternity, all the strings are in place now. We can see the pattern and touch the threads in anticipation of what the finished piece will ultimately look and feel like. We do not have to wait for "some day" to live intimately with God each day. Every string is set. Relationships with God and one another only increase in beautiful depth from here. God established bidirectional access so that on both sides of eternity, we never have to say goodbye.

NEVER GOODBYE

I could fill these pages with reference after reference of Scripture validating the above truth. But it's better to read it for yourself. Instead of copying and pasting the book of Hebrews and both of Paul's letters to the Corinthians, I will illustrate the gospel through my life. I'll be a living letter written by the Holy Spirit.[10]

It is difficult to find language sufficient to describe the value

I place on constant, eternal access to the Father, the Son, and the Holy Spirit. If you have never waited behind innumerable closed doors or sat at the bottom of countless unclimbable stairs, it will be challenging to comprehend the magnitude for me of an open door and straight stairway into God's heart through Jesus. Access is a commodity in the modern world—expected and used without thought. People with disabilities, however, understand the preciousness of access.

In the world's eyes, I have nothing. I live some people's worst-case scenario. I have no physical stamina or mobility. I rely upon the daily help of others for the most basic needs. I plan mundane aspects of life (e.g., getting out of bed, dressing, eating, etc.) months in advance. This requires all my friendships and social experiences to be meticulously planned. Unless friends are willing to help, my social life is regularly sacrificed to my care. There are few spontaneous relational dynamics.

Watch. The gospel is about to be even sweeter. Because of bidirectional access, the Lord and I are free to be spontaneous together. I am welcome in his space always, and he is welcome in my space anytime. We have such a strong relational bond because we can, or as he put it to me once, *I wanted to be close to you, and you said yes.* The desire for closeness is now wholly mutual. We keep saying yes to one another.

I use my limitations as reinforcements of the gospel to my heart. I cannot dress myself, so I allow Jesus to dress me in his righteousness and the Holy Spirit to clothe me in compassion, kindness, humility, gentleness, and patience.[11] When I am stuck outside a door I cannot open, I thank the Father that there is always a door open for me in heaven.[12] When I have to reroute my path around sidewalk construction, I thank Jesus for always making a way for me. Even though I thread my life through restrictive social service systems, God is my spacious place.[13]

Unlike the world's stigma around me, Jesus never patronizes me. He never questions whether I am supposed to be in the room. The Holy Spirit never avoids me in public or chooses to not speak with me because it would take too long to listen. The Father does not tower over me when we converse, even though he fills the cosmos with his glory. We talk eye-to-eye, heart-to-heart. While my voice may be too soft for anyone else to hear, the triune God bends down from heaven to listen for every prayer and love song from my lips. He always hears me.

I have not experienced physical healing yet, but I am not missing out on the Father's kingdom. I do not feel passed by. I am pursued, welcomed, and deeply missed if I forget about my access. From childhood, what I wanted most from Jesus was to be close, and he gave me himself. Since "a longing fulfilled is a tree of life," why are people surprised my heart is not sick? (Prov. 13:12). My hope is secure in my access to God, and Jesus has never once deferred it.

I must take a moment to explain what gospel access is not. When I am spending time with God, I am not using some mystical channel to change my consciousness or for my spirit to leave my body. I am not traveling to heaven. I do not need to *travel* anywhere to enjoy sweet intimacy with the Father and the Son through the Holy Spirit. It grieves me that there are some people who twist gospel access into falsehoods.

There is no ritual, nothing special I do beyond turning my heart to God to say, "I love you, Father/Jesus/Holy Spirit." I have access without any need for striving. This book's title, *Undefiled Access*, emphasizes this access is pure. It is holy, perfect, and eternally made straight. It is undefiled.

INCHES AWAY

Jesus made it possible for me to live inches away from the triune God. One of his favorite nicknames for me is *Inches* because of my delighted determination in using the access he paid for. My habit of burrowing into God's heart also earned me the nickname *Mole*. This second name came with a warning: *You're gonna get yourself stuck in my heart.* The Lord did not add, *And then what are you going to do?*, but he implied it.

Do all my earthly circumstances resolve because I have flawless access to God? No, but they do grow not-so-strangely dim. Do I ignore earthly responsibilities in pursuit of a life with God in heaven now? No, I have the privilege of living as a citizen of heaven while on the earth,[14] hopefully making the earth look more like heaven wherever I go. I live on the earth with access to heaven, and because the Holy Spirit also lives in me, the glory and power of God are available through my life for others.

I am also in love with the written Word of God. Filling my heart and mind with the Bible is like raiding the fridge of God's heart at will. I can reach and eat everything. There is no struggle opening the lid; there is no waiting for someone to make it. The Holy Spirit has beautifully prepared it for me to eat. To borrow the metaphor of Isaiah 55, the bread is wonderful. The milk is delicious. I could never do justice to the wine pouring from God's heart to us in the Bible.[15]

I want to remove a common misconception about spending time in the Scripture. Reading is not the only way to enjoy God's Word. I listen to the Bible more than I read it. A chapter in this book is devoted to the book of Exodus partly because of spiritual warfare I experienced during the writing process. For several weeks, I listened to Exodus on repeat. I'd finish it and immediately start over. By the fourth time through, the Holy Spirit had constructed a strong, protective wall of fire around my heart, and I could finish his assignment.

I encourage those who find reading a challenge to listen to the Bible. The NIV dramatized audio version is my favorite because the voices change with the speakers. We have permission to use all available resources to access God's heart in the Scripture. And just when I think it could not get any better than this, I discover I don't have to eat this feast alone. I can enjoy it with God—in his embrace if I would like.

The best daily-living skills lesson I ever experienced was the Lord's step-by-step instructions on how to get into bed to spend time with him. There is nothing special about my bed, but once you sit for fourteen-plus hours every day, you begin to despise sitting. I did not test God when I launched myself like a leapfrog into bed the first time. I followed directions. The Holy Spirit's communication resembled a dad teaching his kid to ride a bike without training wheels, something close to *You're going to do this, and I won't let you fall.* Hundreds of times later, I have never fallen. He taught me how to do it safely. The only trouble now is that unless God heals my body or somebody comes to help me up, there is no getting away from him. I can't very well run away, can I? This Mole is so stuck.

One afternoon as I lay listening to the book of Deuteronomy, I heard Moses bless the tribe of Benjamin with these words: "Let the beloved of the Lord rest secure in him, for he shields him all day long, and the one the Lord loves rests between his shoulders" (Deut. 33:12). My first thought was, *There is no way I heard that right.* I picked up my phone to check and discovered my ears were correct.

"I knew it!" I exclaimed to the Lord. "I knew your snuggles were biblical."

He never responded; there was not any doubt on his part.

Most spiritual warfare I experience is directed at dislodging the truth of access from my heart. My faith agitates the enemy who uses fear and intimidation to derail trust in God. Since the devil cannot change my access (Jesus secured that) or my heart's purity (the Holy Spirit produces and protects that), the devil attempts to use my sensitivity to the Lord and value for his presence to condemn living from access as false, irreverent, or selfish.

It is a bitter day for Satan when the best weapon he can use against us is our passionate desire to live as close as possible to the Father and to never settle for less. While it is a foretaste for us of the eternal glory coming, it is equally so a foretaste for Satan of his eternal destruction.

IS ACCESS IRREVERENT?

To further celebrate the gospel, I will address the question of irreverence. When I say I can be forever inches away from the Father, you might be tempted to think, *God is holy. You are human. It is irreverent for you to consider yourself always that close.*

True. God is holy, and I am human. I am, however, not irreverent. Jesus's sacrifice makes me holy. I am consecrated, sprinkled clean, and above reproach.[16] I have been given the gift of Jesus's actual righteousness, the real thing.[17] In Jesus, we are holy and can freely come close to him. Access is not presumptive in itself. Presumption and irreverence depend on what we do with our access. It would be one thing if I came close and spit in Jesus's face and quite another altogether if I bow to kiss his feet and say, "I love you."

In providing for nearness, God opened a tender space between our hearts. He does not control how I treat his heart in that space. So I choose to be careful and considerate, doing my part to protect and treasure the gift of our relationship. One dimension of "fearing the Lord" is this attitude of respect and humility. I do not presume I am close because of my goodness, but because of his goodness. I do not assume being close means

I do whatever I please. I am not there to do what I please; I come close to please him.

That said, God is much bigger than I am. I am just a little human creature. He wants me to be close, though, and he helps me stay. Jesus paid dearly for my heart's affection, and he permanently retains the highest rights to it. Repentance is necessary and desirable when I struggle in my weakness, but my righteous status before God never changes. From this place, I gladly receive God's correction of my heart. Jesus's righteousness is never a license to sin.[18] Sin creates distance, even if just for a moment, and distance is not my desire.

ACCESS AND VULNERABILITY

I cried the night of my eighteenth birthday. It is normal to be apprehensive about adulthood, but it is another world to become an adult and not be able to move independently. I have older parents, and their capacity to care for me when I was eighteen was already limited. I had to find ways to be as independent as I could without them. That evening, I told my mom how scared I was.

She comforted me by saying, "I will be here for as long as I can be, but you will grow in intimacy with the Lord. You will learn to depend on God as Father and what it means to be his child."

Four months later, I moved to Arkansas for college on scholarship, hiring assistants to care for me full time. If there was a leave-and-cleave moment in my relationship with God, this was it. Jesus and I soldered our hearts together. The dependence transmission shifted from first to high gear and has remained at full tilt for a decade. At this rate, there must be some holy strength running through my life to keep the engine from breaking. It is certainly not my own strength.

Returning to my parents' house after college graduation, I faced a crisis. I could not find caregivers, and my parents could not provide daily care. I decided to move to Urbana, Illinois, to finish graduate school because of the city's accessibility and the greater availability of services there. I lived seven hours away from my family, trusting the ladies I hired would show up every day. Ten years after my eighteenth birthday, I have tested my mother's words and found them faithful.

Some people perceive me as a type of daredevil intent on pushing the independence envelope for the fun of it. That is an incorrect assumption. The constant vulnerability is exhausting. If I could make it stop, I would. I am hoping to live closer to family someday, but the notion that parents will be forever young and able to care for their adult children with disabilities is wholly inaccurate. The next time someone asks me, "Who takes care of you?" in shocked surprise that I live independently, I will answer, "The Lord of Glory. Who takes care of you?"

I am playing the cards of my life as dealt the best I know how to play them. I hold an ace pair—I am not a naturalist and I live happily divorced from the fear of death. This does not make me careless. On the contrary, the Holy Spirit and I are extremely strategic. His previous instruction proved to be incredibly useful in the times I have to independently get into bed. He taught me in a lower-stakes moment, so I could be successful when it is my only option.

I could waste all my energy exhausting the *what ifs* of the earthly vulnerability I face, or I can rely on my God and allow him to cover it. He is the only one who eternally can anyway. Before I moved to Illinois, I told Jesus I was scared to live so far away and was concerned about the night.

I journaled his response: *I will help you with your fear as you move to Illinois. I will protect you at night. You will be staying in my house, in my chamber, in my arms anyway, and I don't plan to make other arrangements for you.* The last part of his message carried the subtlety of a playful warning intermingled with his promise.

"Yes, Lord," was the only appropriate rejoinder.

The charismatic church likes miracles. Well, the greatest miracle I've experienced to date was how God took a physically immobile girl who was afraid to sleep at night for much of her life and moved her hours from her family twice. In this pressurized crucible, he taught her how to live from the molten wealth of his gospel night and day.

The disability community values access like silver and gold, and Spirit-filled congregations are more likely to teach this component of the gospel. But disabled people avoid charismatic spaces like they avoid the nuisance of inaccessible spaces. Rather than perceiving our faith as the new and living way of access to the Father, they interpret it as another reinforcement of the barriers and stigma in the world.

Few people who acknowledge the access available in Jesus communicate that understanding at wholesale to people with disabilities. We tend to not even share the gospel with them because we overemphasize miraculous healing and do not explain access in God's kingdom.

FAILING TO SEE

In a YouTube clip, a panel of well-known men involved in healing ministry answer a question about how to respond when someone is not healed. Overall, the teaching in the clip is good, and much of it protects people with disabilities. The low point in the clip, though, is when pastor Todd White references someone in the audience.

Talking about growing in faith for healing, Todd says, "I'm growing in the same thing. Otherwise [pointing to the crowd], that boy would be running out of that wheelchair. Right now."[19] Todd's statement sets the stage for a comment pastor Dan Mohler makes a few minutes later.

Referencing Jesus's correction of the disciples in Matthew 17, Dan says,

> He [Jesus] is not saying, "Well, you didn't have faith." What he is saying is it is what you're failing to see because of the ability of your mind to twist.

> But if you see what I see, you'll do what I do. Period. Red letters. [Dan makes eye contact with the boy.] And nothing, Jason. Nothing, Buddy. [Dan turns back to the crowd.] Nothing will be impossible for you. Don't you water that down.[20]

It is good that Dan knew the boy's name and that they had some degree of relationship. Dan humanized Jason before the audience instead of reducing him to only a boy in a wheelchair. I caution against pointing out disabled people when we preach if we do not have their permission. If Todd pointed me out like that, the embarrassment and pressure of the moment would have made me want to disappear through the floor.

It is also not wise to publicly voice our unsatisfied desire for someone to be healed, especially toward a young person. Jason's heart cannot do anything productive with Todd's statement. Todd can be unsatisfied that Jason is not healed, but Todd needs to keep those feelings between himself and the Lord. I cannot see into Todd's heart and choose to believe his heart was pure. He likely acted out of ignorance, unaware there was no protection for Jason's heart in his words. While God's healing power is always available, Jason cannot anchor his hope in the reversal of his earthly circumstances. It is not a strong enough foundation.

The deeper loss in this clip is neither Todd nor Dan reminded Jason of his access to God. Because they only addressed Jason from the lens of physical healing, they did not see the touchpoint between disability and access in the gospel. Dan and Todd teach access to Jesus and the Father through the Holy Spirit. Much to the Lord's amusement, I usually cannot make it through two minutes of a Dan Mohler message before conviction settles heavy, and I turn it off, saying, "Okay, Mr. Mohler. I get it. I'll go 'be with him.'" But I've never heard Dan teach access toward someone who has a disability. The barriers in our ministry indeed come from a failure to see.

Todd's statement made me want to disappear, but Dan's statement made me want to crawl through my phone into that room shouting, "Wait, Mr. Mohler, please don't leave it there! Explain his access!" It would have taken ten seconds for Dan to publicly tell Jason something like, "Remember you have full access to Jesus right now and can be with him anytime you want. Nothing is in your way. Don't water the gifts of healing down, but do not ever water down your access either."

I hope this is not earth-shattering news, but people with disabilities need more than healing. We need everyday access to our Creator. If the charismatic church does not prioritize this truth, the lies of the world remain the only avenue to find "freedom." It is time to intentionally disciple into access. To do otherwise is to shortchange the disability community from all that is available in Jesus. And not only them, but also entire generations of people who unknowingly thirst for an intimate relationship with the God of heaven and earth. How will they know if no one tells them?

SO WORTHY

In charismatic Christianity, I find an everyday God, not a someday God. I am undone by the beauty of his accessible gospel. It is unlike anything else available across the religions of the world. I am a gentile woman, probably descended from a pagan Germanic tribe somewhere in present-day Europe. From that vantage point, there are moments when I look around me in absolute wonder. I am both humbled and delighted to merely be invited.

How did I get grafted into all the promises of Israel and become, with them, the purchased possession of the one true God?[21] How did I inherit his bidirectional presence with my heart functioning like his dwelling place? I look toward Jesus in amazement and ask, "Are you sure you want me here? Are you sure I get to stay? Are you sure we get to be so close?"

Then my vision refocuses, and everything becomes as clear as glass once again. I see Jesus the Lamb of God, who takes away my sin and the sin of the world, dwelling with the Father in the center of heaven's worship.[22] I remember there is a new covenant, and the way has been eternally set for all to come home. One reminder of the scars on Jesus's feet silences my questions. Then the only thing left to do is join with heaven's song to sing, "My God, you are so worthy."

CHAPTER 2

Lovesick for the Bleeding Healer

Those scars on Jesus's feet are important for access and healing. I believe in supernatural healing through the power of Jesus's death and resurrection. When I explain unproductive healing ministry practices in later chapters, I do not want anyone to misinterpret me saying healing does not, or should not, happen. Such a belief would be sad in light of all Jesus paid for on the cross.

Jesus is the exact representation of the Father.[23] As this representation, he is the perfect healer because God heals by nature. God connects healing to his name and nature when he declares to Israel, "I am the LORD, who heals you" (Ex. 15:26). The truth that healing comes from his nature fills me with hope because God will be faithful to represent his nature even unto death. Has he not at least proven that much?

SAVIOR AND HEALER

Showcasing the Messiah's role as Savior and Healer, Isaiah prophesies Jesus's crucifixion in these words:

> Surely he took up our pain
>   and bore our suffering,
> yet we considered him punished by God,
>   stricken by him, and afflicted.
> But he was pierced for our transgressions,
>   he was crushed for our iniquities;
> the punishment that brought us peace was on him,
>   and by his wounds we are healed.
> (Isa. 53:4–5)

In his gospel account, Matthew describes Jesus's healing ministry while referencing this prophecy:

> When evening came, many who were demon-possessed were brought to him, and he drove out the spirits with a word and healed all the sick. This was to fulfill what was spoken through the prophet Isaiah:
> "He took up our infirmities
>   and bore our diseases."
> (Matt. 8:16–17)

Matthew interconnects Jesus's healing works with the saving work of the cross. While some Christians separate these roles, Jesus is not divided in his representation of the Father. He is not compartmentalized. Jesus says he is revealing the Father's nature after he heals a man at the pool of Bethesda. Responding to criticism for healing on the Sabbath, Jesus replies, "My Father is always at his work to this very day, and I too am working" (John 5:17). A few verses later, Jesus gives an even more detailed justification for his healing ministry:

> Jesus gave them this answer: "Very truly I tell you, the Son can do nothing by himself; he can do only what he sees his Father doing, because whatever the Father does the Son also does. For the Father loves the Son and shows him all he does. Yes, and he will show him even greater works than these, so that you will be amazed." (John 5:19–20)

Jesus's healing power demonstrates his identity as God's divine Son, who is faithfully obeying and glorifying the Father. But God does not stop at a mere demonstration. Jesus seals the restoration of the cosmos when he dies and resurrects. Speaking of Jesus, Paul writes,

> For God was pleased to have all his fullness dwell in him, and through him to reconcile to himself all things, whether things on earth or things in heaven,

> by making peace through his blood, shed on the cross. (Col. 1:19–20)

The reconciling peace Jesus bought with his blood guarantees everything in the world can, and will be, restored to how God intended when he first made it: a perfect creation free of sin, death, decay, and pain. Jesus uniquely possesses this re-creational authority; his sacrifice is the only pathway to wholeness.

The healing debate in the church focuses on whether Jesus's creational restoration refers to the future, the present, or both. Both is the biblical answer. There will be a final fulfillment of Jesus's shed blood when he returns.[24] Until then, Jesus's inaugurated kingdom remains accessible, and one of the ways we experience this kingdom is through miracle healing. Such healings have occurred throughout history across the globe to this day. They serve as tangible reinforcements of what Jesus accomplished at the cross and the place he occupies above all creation.

Jesus contextualizes his last earthly instructions to his disciples based on his authority over the cosmos:

> All authority in heaven and on earth has been given to me. Therefore go and make disciples of all nations, baptizing them in the name of the Father and of the Son and of the Holy Spirit, and teaching them to obey everything I have commanded you. And surely I am with you always, to the very end of the age. (Matt. 28:18–20)

Disciples obey *some things* Jesus commanded, right? Not right. Disciples obey *everything*. Among the commands Jesus's disciples obey and teach are his instructions to demonstrate the kingdom of God through the miraculous. Jesus commanded his first disciples to "heal the sick, raise the dead, cleanse those who have leprosy, drive out demons. Freely you have received; freely give" (Matt. 10:8). See comparative passages throughout the Gospels with a similar command and authority given.[25]

As fellow disciples of Jesus, we are on shaky ground when we say some commands from Jesus apply to us while others do not. By that measuring line, we could end up minimizing the authority of the Sermon on the Mount. I am not interested, however, in debating healing ministry differences between us and Jesus's first followers. Those books are already available, and honestly, my heart does not care much about those arguments.

THE ARGUMENT FROM AFFECTION

I've been asked why I believe healing is always possible through Jesus's cross when my experience does not align with that belief. More specifically, does holding a belief that contradicts my circumstances make God appear inconsistent?

No. My circumstances do not contradict God or Scripture. I hold the truth of Scripture much higher than my experiences, as I should. Not experiencing healing does not change anything about Calvary's power to accomplish it. Jesus died. Jesus suffered before and on the cross so all could live and all could be healed. It is finished.

I respect Jesus's suffering too much to change my mind about his heart toward my own. My value for Jesus's sacrifice carries far greater weight than any circumstance. I've never heard anyone make an argument for healing in the atonement—a theological term for Jesus's salvific death—based on affection for Jesus, so I'll try it. The argument from affection goes like this:

1. Jesus is precious.[26]
2. Jesus suffered a painful, torturous death.[27]
3. His death provided for the reconciliation of humanity to God and restoration of the created world now to eternity.[28]

Conclusion: if I reduce the outcome of Jesus's death to anything less than point three, then I sell his suffering and his worth short of their value.

The cross is too high a purchase price to be unproductive. I will not cheapen its power. Asking me to renege my faith in atonement-based healing is close to suggesting I join the mockers and spit in Jesus's face.[29]

Jesus gently taught me about his crucifixion, yet every new layer of knowledge remained a high-impact moment. Not because of the violence itself, but because the violence was personalized—directed toward a person I know. He is not only my savior on that cross. He is my brother, my friend, my treasure. He is the most dearly beloved of my whole soul. It is enough for me to think about what happened to his feet—and I have thought long about it.

REMEMBERING HIS DEATH

I see six-year-old Elizabeth in a Catholic church foyer staring at a marble scene of Mary holding Jesus's dead body just removed from the cross. The scene arrested my attention as I considered Mary's pain.

Dad was behind me, and I said, "Daddy, it must have been really hard for Mary to watch Jesus die."

"Oh yes," he whispered.

I've carried this memory for more than twenty years. The scene symbolizes my argument from affection; I will never depreciate Jesus's costly gift for my own sake.

I remember learning a *scourge* is not just a whip when I found a footnote describing it in my children's Bible. Surprised and horrified, I discovered that beyond a sharp piece of leather, there was bone and metal embedded too. I remember crawling on the stage steps at church investigating the Good Friday display before service. I held one of the nails in my tiny, contracted hand, and thought, *That's a really big nail*, while pondering how something like this went through Jesus's wrist. I touched the coins from the open bag of money representing Judas's betrayal as my young heart grappled with the significance of such a choice against such a person.

I know exactly where I was when I understood crucifixion meant death by slow asphyxiation due to not being able to exhale. At that moment, I realized Jesus knew what it felt like to not be able to breathe, and we shared this experience. He stopped breathing so I could breathe.

The argument from affection reached its pinnacle after I read Christian author Lee Strobel's mini-book, *The Case for Easter*, at age nineteen. The first chapter discusses the crucifixion. I marshaled all my resolve to finish that chapter, its contents now branded into my mind. Jesus is more intimately acquainted with muscle spasms, nerve pain, and restricted joints from six-plus hours of his life than I have ever been in all of mine.

Until then, I had entertained an internal rebuttal to the platitude "Jesus has gone through everything we go through." I had thought, *Jesus never lived in a body like mine, so he could not possibly know what it is like.* After that chapter, I repented and shut my mouth forever on the subject of Jesus knowing what I endure. My God understands pain, which gives me hope in circumstances I do not always understand. Moreover, he was willing to suffer pain so I could be healed. That is all I need to know.

The cross does not guarantee everyone will be physically healed before Jesus's return, but there is always an open door for the possibility. Always. Because Jesus died. My circumstances are irrelevant in the magnitude of his sacrifice. The biblical support for this position is robust, and the argument from affection is final.

LIVING FROM CONTEXT

The argument from affection is both justification for faith in supernatural healing and a protection against offense while I await healing. I've never been angry at the Lord for not healing my body. Sad, yes. Confused, yes. But not angry. The Holy Spirit has lived in me for as long as I remember, and he graciously shares his love for Jesus with my heart. God also gave me a specific skill.

Each time I complete the Gallup CliftonStrengths inventory, my number one strength never fluctuates: *Context*. Gallup's description of people with this strength is an exact summary of my inner life:

> You look back. You look back because that is where the answers lie. You look back to understand the present. From your vantage point the present is unstable, a confusing clamor of competing voices. It is only by casting your mind back to an earlier time, a time when the plans were being drawn up, that the present regains its stability. The earlier time was a simpler time. It was a time of blueprints. As you look back, you begin to see these blueprints emerge. You realize what the initial intentions were.[30]

I have no intellectual or emotional grid for questions like "If God is good, why did he let this happen?" Now, I hear Satan's ready accusations against God in my life, but none of them are any good. I cannot decontextualize God's goodness from the expansive blueprint he created, suffered into, and will forever sustain. From the Tree of Life through a tree of suffering back to the Tree of Life, God's context is consistent and a trustworthy framework from which to live no matter what comes. I understand the story. Why would I be angry at a God who allowed himself to be broken so I could know him today, tomorrow, and forever?

One reason for spiritual confusion among people in the church today is that few people are taught the larger story of God in the Bible, and so they have no grounding for how the present situates within that framework. It is important, for example, to teach how to minister in the gifts of the Holy Spirit, but we must cement that teaching in God's bigger story and his long-term intentions toward humanity. The biblical story is foundational to life in the kingdom of God.

The Bible brims over with accounts of people whose suffering God redeemed for a great purpose. Joseph's story is particularly salient in this regard. His half brothers sell him into slavery at age seventeen. After initial success working for the captain of the guard in Egypt, he is falsely accused of attempted rape and thrown into prison. These circumstances set the stage for Joseph's capacity to save Egypt and the rest of the ancient world from death by famine. Joseph eventually understands this.

He tells his brothers when they reunite in Egypt, "And now, do not be distressed and do not be angry with yourselves for selling me here, because it was to save lives that God sent me ahead of you" (Gen. 45:5). I was highly favored to have early access to this context-building story and the others like it saturating the Scripture. They saved me from the added sorrow of bitterness toward God.

At age ten or eleven, I heard a sermon on the parting of the Red Sea in Exodus 14. After describing the panicked reactions of the Israelites as the Egyptian army streamed down upon them, the pastor said, "God is looking for people who will worship him on this side of the sea, before they see the victory." As he spoke, relief flooded my heart. I thought, *Oh, that's what God wants. I can do that.*

I could do so little of what I, or others, wanted me to do, and I felt joy in learning God's expectations were within my capacity. He wanted worship and trust; I could choose that response. While this understanding did not prevent some Red Sea moments or the Holy Spirit intercepting my heart a few times on the road back to Egypt, it motivated me. Looking at my life so far, its arc bends toward worship on the near side of the sea.

AN AVAILABLE GOD

The biblical story is the background for the colorful foreground of a relationship I did not choose first.[31] I know the main character in the story. God has every right to say to me exactly what he said to Israel: "What have I done to you? How have I burdened you? Answer me" (Mic. 6:3). How can I be angry at a God who has been intentionally tender to me since my earliest awareness of him, who lets me curl up on his shoulder every night? That is an impossible sell.

To be clear, God is not upset with us if we are mad at him. He has broad shoulders and is more than willing to sit with us in our pain. I am also not being flippant with the pain in this world. I have endured searing tragedy in my life and the lives of people precious to me. Grief is real; pain is real. But I do not attack the Lord's character over it. For thirty seconds once, I considered whether it was abusive to have all power to heal me, to have the desire to heal me, and to not do it. That sounds bad on the surface. But my heart decided Jesus would never abuse me. He is just not like that. I've spent too much time with him to think his heart works that way. Intimacy annihilates the option.

But we cannot access a loving, faithful response in suffering until we have allowed our hearts to be undone by the knowledge that God is intimately familiar with pain—his, ours, and everyone else's. I am not angry at the Lord for not healing me yet, but I have cried in his arms. Many times in prayer, I've settled my little face up against his face, looked into his beautiful eyes, and said: "So . . . I don't get it, and I don't know what to do." I do not avoid the incongruence.

PURSUIT AND RECEIPT

The hardest healing in the Bible for me to read is the woman healed from bleeding. Her life mirrors mine. No doctor on earth can heal me. I reached the limits of medicine at ten years old when doctors said they had no solution to loosen a muscle group in my legs that prevented walking. If they altered these muscles, I would lose the strength to stand completely. My body relies on the stability of the contracted muscles to compensate for the weakness of others to stand.

I identify with the woman's determination to touch Jesus for healing. There is no other option for her, and she is fiercely pursuing the one course left. She fights through a crowd of people, breaks her culture's purity laws, and receives healing. She got what she pursued. Then, she tries to get away without notice, but Mr. Pursuit had his own plans for her.

Many people use this healing to tell disabled people they have to "want it more" or "pursue better" to be healed. This religious jargon comes from people who do not understand what it means to seek healing. Only those who have never suffered in their bodies say such words. I see the element of pursuit and receipt also, which is why it is difficult. I have pursued, yet I am still awaiting the receipt. My heart, though, is set to a different rhythm than chasing my healing. I understand the principle of pursuit in God's kingdom, so I am intentional and specific about what, or rather who, I pursue.

For years, I carried a question in my heart without actually sharing it with Jesus, and one day, I decided to ask: "If that woman can receive healing by pursuing to touch the edge of your clothing, what happens to someone who lays hold of your face?"

I bet if you stay that close, you'll find out was the immediate answer in my heart.

The Lord did not suggest I pursue intimacy with him to be healed. That is not what I heard. When we spend time together, I am not generally thinking about my need for healing. Once, I momentarily forgot I could not stand by myself. I'll never live that one down. He still teases me about it.

His response reinforced the notion that I will obtain what I seek in my pursuit to know him and that the opportunity for healing remains on the table between our hearts. His answer also suggested he will not heal me apart from intimacy between us, which is the opposite emphasis of me chasing intimacy for healing. It is about him, not me. I should've never expected it to be otherwise, and I am not upset. All I ever wanted was to be close anyway, whether I am healed or not.

We must take our questions to the Lord. Although we may not always find a clear answer, we will always find him, and he is enough. How many of our burning questions remain kindled because we never started a conversation? It is in these heart-to-heart exchanges that unconditional love is enabled to bloom.

THE JOY OF LOVING

I have an opportunity to make a beautiful choice in response to the difficult circumstances I face. I have the chance to give God, through the Holy Spirit's power, a measure of the love he has shown me back to his own heart. I have the pleasure of loving him unconditionally. God is so worth that kind of love, and he takes much delight in it. Our earthly lives provide an exclusive moment to love God in pain.

It thrills the Lord's heart, and it terrifies the evil one, when we face trouble and our response to God stays consistent, stays tender. I cherish the delight in the Lord's eyes when I tell him how much I love him and trust him amid the pain. There is unspeakable joy in returning to his heart a little of what he has poured out over ours. It is a pleasure nobody should want to miss.

I maintain that attitude because of my infallible willpower. No, I am so kidding. I maintain it because God is good to me and strong for me. One time, I was asking the Father about my healing, frustrated my body was inhibiting my plans.

After waiting awhile, I heard the Father say, *Why don't you go love my Son and forget about the pain?*

Slightly surprised by the abruptness of that sweet invitation, I replied, "Yes, Father. I'll go do that." Heaven's priorities are often far above our frustrations.

My endgame is to make the cross sweet for Jesus, to be as good to him as he enables me to be. That is my blueprint. All other goals, desires, and plans are subservient to this pursuit. Like everyone, I face weakness in my humanity. But I pursue excellence toward God's heart because the gospel sets us free toward excellence.

"Making it sweet" means choosing intimacy, obedience, and surrender to the fullest extent possible while gladly repenting when I do not choose correctly. It means remaining loyal at cost. Believing God heals supernaturally and choosing to trust his character in that are matters of great, personal loyalty to me. So also is not being angry when I suffer. I cannot be affectionate to Jesus and angry at the same time.

We all have this choice. Will we love God and believe him at a cost, or will we live offended and self-righteous, changing God's story to make it more palatable to our circumstances?

CHAPTER 3

Little Seed

Some days, the cost is higher than others. On my worst day, my body feels like every muscle fiber makes a pact to see how far they can hyperextend and contract, each one hoping to outmatch the rest. Never mind that I need them all to work together; they much prefer to fight against each other. My muscles never rest, not even in sleep.

After a rough day, I texted a friend, "I very much want to be healed, my friend. The smaller issues are the symptoms of a larger problem that compounds on itself. I am weary tonight of all the pain. I believe Jesus wants to heal."

She replied, "I cannot imagine how much you desire this. I'm praying for total healing for you." A few messages later, she added: "I just see him [Jesus] cradling you. He has his hold on you in tender strength."

In the comfort of this prophetic picture, I carried the pain to the Lord's heart that night, and I heard the Holy Spirit whisper to my heart, *It's gonna be okay, Little Seed.*

The Lord had never called me that nickname before, and I recognized the allusion: "Unless a kernel of wheat falls to the ground and dies, it remains only a single seed. But if it dies, it produces many seeds" (John 12:24). I could infer the rest of the message. The Holy Spirit said in not so many words, "I know the pain is bad, but yield again. Lay your life back down and trust me with what I will produce through it."

Okay, I yield again and again—into the ground this Little Seed goes, trusting there will be a harvest if she does not give up. This harvest is not my healing. It is life produced as I submit to the Holy Spirit. Here's the harvest I'm referencing:

> Whoever sows to please their flesh, from the flesh will reap destruction; whoever sows to please the Spirit, from the Spirit will reap eternal life. Let us not become weary in doing good, for at the proper time we will reap a harvest if we do not give up. Therefore, as we have opportunity, let us do good to all people, especially to those who belong to the family of believers. (Gal. 6:8–10)

In the previous chapter, I shared how Jesus's sacrifice provides for all healing, including mine. But at its core, the gospel is not about our circumstances. It is about God, and the length he went to redeem a humanity that rejected him because he is good. Redemption is what good, perfect lovers do. To this end, Jesus is the big seed. We are the little seeds, following in his footsteps of sacrificial love to showcase what God's heart is like to the world.

THE PURPOSE OF THE MIRACULOUS

Miracles provide a precious opportunity to encounter God's heart as he moves in love toward people. The experiences, though, are not the goal. The ultimate aim, the *telos*, of miracles is the confirmation of the gospel. Like how the *telos* of human sexuality to bring children into the world protects the beautiful experience of sexual intimacy, so also miracle power is stewarded and protected when it remains connected to its gospel-confirming purpose. The experience is good, but it is not the end function.

Jesus's healing ministry validated his sonship. He tells his audience,

> Do not believe me unless I do the works of my Father. But if I do them, even though you do not believe me, believe the works, that you may know and understand that the Father is in me, and I in the Father. (John 10:37–38)

Along with affirming Jesus's identity, the healings agreed with prophetic signals of the Messiah's coming. Isaiah places ultra-emphasis on the Messiah's healing works:

> And when he comes, he will open the eyes of the blind
> > and unplug the ears of the deaf.
> The lame will leap like a deer,
> > and those who cannot speak will sing for joy!
> Springs will gush forth in the wilderness,
> > and streams will water the wasteland.
> > (Isa. 35:5–6 NLT)

After Jesus ascended to heaven and gave the Holy Spirit to his disciples, miracles accompanied the proclamation of Jesus as the Messiah in Jerusalem, Samaria, and throughout the world.[32] Where the gospel is announced, miracles occur. Throughout the Scripture, we find a duet between power and proclamation.

In a letter to the Thessalonian church, Paul celebrates this duet:

> For we know, brothers and sisters loved by God, that he has chosen you, because our gospel came to you not simply with words but also with power, with the Holy Spirit and deep conviction. You know how we lived among you for your sake. You became imitators of us and of the Lord, for you welcomed the message in the midst of severe suffering with the joy given by the Holy Spirit. (1 Thess. 1:4–6)

Paul assures these new believers of their security in God's family by the evidence of miracle power and the Holy Spirit's conviction when they heard the gospel. Paul also emphasizes the relationship between God's power and proclamation to the Corinthian church,

> My message and my preaching were not with wise and persuasive words, but with a demonstration of the Spirit's power, so that your faith might not rest on human wisdom, but on God's power. (1 Cor. 2:4–5)

The gospel-confirming role of the miraculous is illustrated in Acts 14 when Paul is preaching to a crowd in Lystra with Barnabas:

> In Lystra there sat a man who was lame. He had been that way from birth and had never walked. He listened to Paul as he was speaking. Paul looked directly at him, saw that he had faith to be healed and called out, "Stand up on your feet!" At that, the man jumped up and began to walk. (Acts 14:8–10)

This healing could be read as someone having faith for healing. The end. But such a reduction ignores the deeper exchange occurring. This man listened to Paul. What was Paul talking about that he was so drawn to? From the passage details plus his missionary trips and letters, I doubt Paul was discussing how to get healed provided the correct modicum of faith.

No, Paul was preaching Jesus as Messiah and Lord. He was preaching Christ crucified as the way open for his gentile audience to enter Israel's fulfilled salvation. Later, Paul tells the same audience, "We are bringing you good news, telling you to turn from these worthless things to the living God, who made the heavens and the earth and the sea and everything in them" (Acts 14:15).

When the man hears the gospel, his heart moves toward the Messiah for healing. It is this faith that Paul encounters when their eyes meet. Paul realizes this guy is tracking with him. They are seeing the same Jesus. And yes, there is a powerful miracle to validate the truth of who Jesus is.

A CATALYST FOR MASS SALVATIONS . . .

Three of the four specific healings in Acts involve someone who cannot walk.[33] These miracles are a catalyst for the salvation of many people. After Peter and John heal a man at the temple and share Jesus as Messiah, 2,000 people become disciples of Jesus.[34] When Peter prays for Aeneas, paralyzed for eight years, he is healed, and Luke tells us, "All those who lived in Lydda and Sharon saw him and turned to the Lord" (Acts 9:35). Moreover, when Philip takes the gospel to Samaria, Luke summarizes that "many who were paralyzed or lame were healed. So there was much joy in that city" (Acts 8:7–8).

The emphasis on healing paralysis in Acts does not mean that those were the only types of conditions healed. Other healing summaries do not mention specific conditions.[35] The pattern we find in Acts, though, is that God uses more dramatic healings, like paralysis, to bring people to salvation at scale.

I never noticed the relationship between healing and mass salvation until my sister Rachel reported it to me while taking an Acts class for her ministry degree at the International House of Prayer of Kansas City University. "Every time a paralyzed person is healed in Acts, there is revival!" she exclaimed. Talk about a lightbulb moment. I wondered how I missed that delicious detail in twenty years of charismatic faith.

The professor who connected these dots for Rachel and me, Dr. Wes Adams, experienced quadriplegia himself. Dr. Adams forever altered the angle I take on miracle healing. I understand my place in God's larger story much better now. My circumstances are an open door to launch revival. This truth sets my heart free to trust God for healing and anchors my motive to something higher than myself. Should I stand someday before eternity, I will be standing for Jesus's great name.

Dr. Adams is walking with Jesus in heavenly places now. The night I learned of his passing, I was writing the final pages of this book's first draft. I felt a momentary stab of loneliness. He was one of a few quadriplegics as passionate as I am about the Holy Spirit's presence and power, and he is not paralyzed anymore. I considered dedicating the book to him, but Dr. Adams would have supported who I chose instead.

Dr. Adams also taught revival history. God did not take a nap at the end of Acts and suddenly wake up to do miracles in the twenty-first century. Charismatics sometimes talk about the miraculous from a perspective of novelty, as if God waited for us to be alive so he can move in power again. While we are valuable to the Lord in our generations, we are not overly important. God has been displaying power through the name of Jesus to confirm the gospel for thousands of years before any of us breathed. I am comforted and emboldened by the invitation to humbly join the back of the line and participate in the ancient, long-standing desires of his heart.

In *Miracles Today: The Supernatural Work of God in the Modern World,* New Testament scholar Dr. Craig Keener likewise reminds us of miracle activity throughout church history to this day. He lists records of healing and deliverance miracles most of which accompanied conversion to Christianity. Keener summarizes,

> Miracles are associated with the earliest missionaries who evangelized England, Scotland, Ireland, Germany, Persia, and elsewhere. In some more recent periods as well, healing has been associated with Jesus's message coming to new peoples—for example, during the predominantly Presbyterian revival in Korea in the early twentieth century. By 1981, a thesis that surveyed more than 350 other theses reported more accounts of miracles in new mission contexts than the author had room to use. Healing remains a major feature in Majority World evangelism.[36]

Keener both initiates and answers a common question Western Spirit-filled believers ask: Why are there so many more healings in the Majority World than in Western culture? The gospel is going forth outside of the West. The church is growing fastest in the Majority World, so it makes sense they are experiencing the dramatic, miraculous signs.

Miracles are still happening in the West, as Keener also documents (see chapter 6). This is a great moment to be a Western charismatic believer. Western society is now predominantly post-Christian, and the West will see more of the miraculous as God's people rise to share the gospel and break new ground again for God's kingdom. We have an opportunity to learn from our brothers and sisters throughout the globe and share Jesus like they do at all costs.

. . . AND PERSECUTION

The miraculous is costly. In Scripture and life, it often comes with significant persecution. After healing the man at Lystra, Paul and Barnabas struggle to restrain a rioting crowd from sacrificing to them as supposed Greek gods. In the end, the riot turns south. Those who oppose Paul and Barnabas's gospel message agitate the crowd and convince them to stone Paul until everyone thinks he is dead. They drag his body outside the city. When the believers encircle Paul, he gets up and returns to Lystra.[37]

This example is one of many throughout the Gospels and Acts of persecution alongside the miraculous confirmation of

Jesus as Lord. Here is a list of this dynamic playing out in the New Testament:

- Jesus is persecuted for his many Sabbath healings (e.g., Mark 3:1–6; Matt. 12:9–14; Luke 6:6–11; John 5).
- The religious authorities seek to kill Jesus and Lazarus after Jesus raises Lazarus from the dead (John 12:9–11).
- Peter and John are thrown into prison and threatened by the Sanhedrin after healing a man in Jesus's name at the temple and then proclaiming Jesus as Messiah (Acts 4:1–22).
- Jealous of the many people joining the church because of the gospel's miraculous confirmation, the Sanhedrin arrests the apostles. When they are supernaturally released from prison, they go to the temple to continue sharing about Jesus. When arrested again, they are beaten and threatened (Acts 5:12–42).
- Stephen was known in the church for signs and wonders and for sharing the gospel with wisdom. This precipitates the conflict leading to his arrest by false accusation, his defense before the Sanhedrin, and martyrdom (Acts 6:8–7:60).
- Because of persecution in Jerusalem, Philip shares the gospel in Samaria, accompanied by miracle healings and deliverance (Acts 8:1–8).

- Paul is stoned at Lystra when a riot is started over a healing miracle (Acts 14:8–20).

Paul comments on the dual reality of the Holy Spirit's power and suffering in the letter to the Thessalonians referenced earlier. Alongside power and conviction, the Thessalonian church "welcomed the message in the midst of severe suffering with the joy given by the Holy Spirit" (1 Thess. 1:6). If we were to interview brothers and sisters across the globe who face persecution for their faith, we would find the same dynamic. The people ministering in the Holy Spirit's power and those who receive miracles are often the first ones on the hit list because Satan is motivated to eliminate testimony to the gospel. Although we have every reason to celebrate the gift of God's miraculous power, it is sobering to consider the weighty responsibility of carrying testimony to Jesus's name and power in our very bodies.

At this stage of God's story, glory and suffering are interwoven. We must keep our perspective and expectations in alignment with this truth so we do not surrender to offense. Higher than the cost of living and dying for Jesus, offense is an expensive purchase no one can afford.

If our hearts are offended when circumstances turn out differently than we would like, the question to ask ourselves is "What are you living for?" or better "Who are you living for?" If I am living for myself, then yes, I have every right to be offended when I do not get what I prefer. But if I am living to reflect the image of my God, then it does not matter what happens to me. I am not a Christian because Jesus heals. I am a Christian because Jesus is Lord.

The above statement is what differentiates a Spirit-filled understanding of the gospel from the prosperity gospel. Some conflate these divergent beliefs to criticize charismatic faith. Healing is available, but the gospel is not a means to escape suffering or to arrange a comfortable life. The gospel exists so we can live out our created purpose to represent God's heart on the earth, including his desire and power to heal.

After I prayed for his healing, a friend once said, "It's amazing that you don't let where you are limit how God can use you."

I wasn't sure how to respond. If I cannot pray for someone's healing because I'm upset there is no healing for me yet, what kind of sister am I? The order of the day is to lay our lives down for one another. It would never cross my mind to not pray for my brother. There is some dissonance in my circumstances, but I trust God to use that for his purposes and glory.

DISSONANCE

Spirit-filled believers often treat me like nothing useful can happen in my life until my body is whole or like the fact that I am not healed is the worst of tragedies. Those are both false perspectives. God is using my life for his purposes, and he revels in my obedience.

Over one hundred people have worked for me as personal assistants (PA) throughout the past decade. In the last four years, a majority of them were not Christians. I am an equal-opportunity employer, and I've loved knowing all of them.

The ladies who work for me quickly learn three things:

1. Elizabeth believes Jesus is deeply real, and they spend a lot of time together.
2. Elizabeth believes Jesus heals people because she prays for us when we don't feel well.
3. Elizabeth believes that she can hear God's heart for people because she tells us what she hears is on Jesus's heart for us.

All have an intimate window into my life. They see me at my worst when I am not living in the truth of the gospel. They see me repent and ask for forgiveness. Through it all, they see I believe in a tangible, available God.

One of them routinely enjoyed it. After I explained I'm spending time with Jesus, not sleeping, when she found me in my bed for her weekly afternoon shift, she believed me. If I was in bed when she came, she would say, "I know you're faking it, Elizabeth. You're not asleep." Without fail, I'd burst into confirming giggles that I was not asleep, which motivated her to keep making the same accurate observation. It didn't help that the Holy Spirit was only too happy to add his own commentary to the situation. Pretty soon, I'd start laughing when I heard the front door open.

My relationship with God doesn't stop when my PAs come

in my door. Case in point, I sat at the table while one of them made dinner, attempting to resist a conversation the Holy Spirit wanted to continue. It was the wrong move.

He whispered to my heart, *You invited me over. You can't just kick me out.*

I laughed, and of course, she asked me what was funny. Thank you, Holy Spirit, for throwing me right off the worldview cliff. I explained how I believe Jesus lives in me, I can "hear" him, and sometimes he is funny. I even told her what he said to me. I differentiated this for her from an auditory delusion, but I am sure she had no reference for the concept. Most people don't.

Another time the Holy Spirit moved my heart to pray for one of them when she was hurting. She lay on the floor in pain, waiting for me to finish a project before bed. This was the same PA who'd tease me about my afternoon snuggles with the Lord. I asked for her permission to pray, took her hand, and prayed a simple prayer that she would experience the Father's love and healing. I felt warmth move through my arm and hand. She looked at me and said the pain was gone. We were both amazed. I explained that was Jesus, not me, and shared how much he loved her. Over a year later, I prayed for her again about something else.

This time, she asked, "Do you remember when you prayed for me that one time and the pain went away?"

"Yes," I said.

"I would like to be able to do that, but I would be afraid."

"I was afraid, but Jesus helped me do it anyway," I replied. "And it wasn't something I did. It was Jesus's power that comes through relationship with him."

It's curious that a PA, who treated my relationship with Jesus as real as I do, experienced his power. I often shared about Jesus with her because she was open to listening. I've prayed for many people, and that is the only time I've felt power go through my arm. She did not yield her heart to Jesus that night, but I trust God uses my life to plant truth and hope in the hearts of those around me.

THE MASTER STRATEGIST

The best, though, is when we see the harvest. I received a text one night from a girl who helped me with food at the dorm cafeteria during graduate school. I shared a simple prophetic word with her, speaking life and Jesus's perspective over her heart. One Sunday morning, I saw her walking on the other side of the street.

After we waved at each other and she turned away, I yelled her name across the street at the top of my lungs and added, "Jesus really loves you!" The Holy Spirit must have hijacked my vocal cords. I rarely yell.

Two years later, she got my number through a mutual friend and texted me she had given her life to Jesus. We met for coffee, and she shared how Jesus used me and another disabled student she worked for to woo her heart. I learned then that she was raised in another faith and never had the opportunity to find out about Jesus until college. What a beautiful time for them to meet!

Stories like the ones above all happened within the last few years, and if I'd been healed prior, none of them would have occurred. My circumstances were the soil from which they developed. While I do not enjoy having a disability, I can see God working and moving his story forward. Every moment of pain is unilaterally worth it if people come to know Jesus in its wake. That is not a high-level sacrifice. It is basic Christianity, a servant who knows her duty.[38]

I treasure the gift of miracle healing as an equal opportunity to confirm the gospel before an unbelieving world. As much as my life bears witness in suffering, so also would the restoration of my body. God is glorified whenever we showcase Jesus to the world—in suffering and liberation. Both are equally valid. I wonder what the ladies who work for me would do if they came into my apartment one morning and found me sitting on the couch waiting for them.

I've been planning my healing party since I was a little girl. The longer I wait, the longer my guest list grows. At this rate, I'll have to rent a wedding venue. The more people I meet, the more who may yet taste Jesus's miracle power in my life. God's heart is for healing, and he is the master strategist.

God waited for Joseph to end up in an Egyptian prison so that he could save the ancient Near East from famine. He waited for Pharaoh's army to pursue Israel before he parted the Red Sea.

God waited for the Roman Empire to create a network of navigable roads before Jesus came so that his disciples could bring the gospel hope to Israel and the nations. Jesus waited for Lazarus to die and be in the grave for three days so that on account of that resurrection, people would trust him as the Messiah and be primed to accept the soon-after testimony of his own resurrection. God is strategic. This is not my story or my game. I happily yield to be one word on his page or one chess piece in his hand.

That sounds poetic on paper, but when the grit, grind, and pressure of our circumstances surround us, how do we keep looking back at God with another yes? We see that God meets our gaze with his own yes. God's yes is to always come close. He is the master comforter.

THE MASTER COMFORTER

It all comes back to a gospel of perfect access. I am waiting for healing, but I do not live with any sense of missing out on the privileges of the kingdom. I revel in them all. My cup spills over with the delight of my God.

As this Little Seed goes into the ground, I allow the Lord his right as first and ultimate comforter. I allow him to love me. No matter how poorly I sleep at night or how much pain I am in, the Holy Spirit can always find some way to be sweet to me. One of his strategies is whispering to my heart in the mornings, *I bet I can still get a smile out of you.* If he is keeping score in this version of "Honey, do you love me?", then I am losing badly.

In 2018, I endured a grueling surgery. I stayed in the hospital for ten days and in a nursing facility for nineteen more. Physically and psychologically, recovery from that surgery was one of the hardest seasons. The worst part was not being able to leave the facility, even though I could see the dirt road leading to my parents' house from my window. (I'd returned to Kansas City for that summer before finalizing my permanent move to Illinois.) After I stopped the pain medicine that made me anxious, I resolved to be okay because I could go to my other home—my Father's presence. I am grateful the Holy Spirit spent the previous nine months burning the truth of access to the Father and Jesus into my heart. I needed all that context about this everyday God.

A few weeks before the surgery, he told me, *Let the pain recede into the background of my kindness.* Notice he did not say, "Just use your authority, and there won't be any pain." He knew there would be pain, and he is a good Father to tell me the truth. The pain was intense, but so was his loving-kindness. We talked long after visiting hours were over. Nobody can kick the Holy Spirit out. The content for the argument from affection in the previous chapter came from one of these conversations. He brought me through a series of memories, showing me how he designed my heart to respond to Jesus. I lay in a hospital bed with three tubes coming out of my body, weeping and listening.

Sometimes when the pain was bad, the Lord would just hold me. Sometimes he would make me laugh.

One of the nurses would tell me good night, saying, "Sweet dreams. I hope he's cute."

I would never call the Lord "cute." But nevertheless, I'd laugh and internally protest, *Oh, please don't encourage Jesus to show up in my dreams. I'm having enough trouble handling his delight while I'm awake.* My protests did not work. Jesus showed up in a dream with all his delight. He had a grand time using *his* access to my heart over those days, whether I was asleep or awake.

I have a working theory that part of the reason the triune God made me was to laugh at the Holy Spirit's jokes. He told me a great Bible joke in that hospital bed. *How many disciples does it take to change a lightbulb?*

"I don't know. How many?" I asked.

Two.

"Why two?"

I tossed up options for several minutes before the Holy Spirit said, *You won't guess it.*

Not one to be denied, I kept guessing.

It wasn't until I quietly listened that I heard him say, *Someone has to change the lightbulb, but someone else has to catch a fish and take the lightbulb out of its mouth.*

Yeah, I never would've guessed that. The Holy Spirit assured me the laughter he got (and is still getting) out of me over this joke was well worth his investment. But I'm an easy crowd. If you don't know the punch line, read Matthew 17:24–27.

This story is silly, but it is good. I'm almost embarrassed how profoundly moved I am by the fact that the Spirit of God enjoys telling me jokes. He is the best comforter. He longs to cry with us and, if we let him, to turn our tears into laughter. Paul describes the Father as "the God of all comfort" (2 Cor. 1:3). Unlike the comfort of the world, which leaves us numb and washed out, God's comfort leaves us feeling more alive than ever, filled to overflowing with the knowledge of God and his measureless love.

By the time I left the facility, the nurses didn't want me to go. They liked coming into my room because there was so much peace. That's because Mr. Shalom had me so well snuggled in his arms. I got to pray with many of the nurses, sharing the joy of access to God.

I long that the disability community would have the chance to know my beautiful God who reaches out to them each day. I am not some exception to the rule. The Christian faith has always been a gospel of access to God now and forever.

He waits. He waits. He waits. Not to shackle people with disabilities again with the shame and stigma of the world, but to lift them into seats of honor where there is no such thing as rejection. They do not know this, however, and most have learned to assume the worst about Jesus's intentions toward them. Before the disability community will listen to his invitation we bring, we will have to first learn about their culture.

CHAPTER 4

Social Construct or Identity? (Disability Culture Part 1)

To understand disability in the twenty-first century, we need to dip our toes in the waters of philosophy. Don't worry, I won't push us into the deep end. But we need to know the basic definition of a philosophical word—*metaphysics*. *Metaphysics* is the area of philosophy dealing with what is ultimately real or, as *Merriam-Webster* says, "the fundamental nature of reality."[39] Metaphysical questions address the universe's origin and the existence of God as well as human value, purpose, and meaning in life. They represent the core questions everyone must answer in some way. All spiritual questions are metaphysical.

Answers to metaphysical questions determine a person's worldview, like the way building materials determine the structure and design of a house. The friction between disability culture and the Spirit-filled church is the result of our differing worldviews. Rather than engaging in dialogue across these differences, Spirit-filled believers are quick to use their worldview answers as ultimate conversation-stoppers toward disabled people. Imagine a neighbor invites you to dinner at their house. The polite thing to do is knock on the door and wait for it to open, not attempt to break in.

Christianity offers a specific, exclusive set of metaphysics, and that alone is offensive. I am not asking us to change our answers or our worldview. I am asking us to remember that the offense inherent in the gospel does not give us license to be offensive. Before anything else, biblical love is patient and kind. Instead of ramrodding our perspective, let's knock on Western culture's worldview door and learn its interpretation of disability. The normalization of disability is the foundation of this construction.

THE DISABILITY RIGHTS MOVEMENT

In the 1970s, the disability community in the United States began to garner national attention as they birthed what would become known as the Disability Rights Movement. Disability rights leaders successfully organized to promote the passing and enforcement of Section 504 of the Rehabilitation Act of 1973. Section 504, as it is commonly known, was the first legislation mandating accessibility for any entity receiving federal tax dollars. Before this law passed, public transportation, universities, healthcare organizations, and the like were not even basically accessible. As a famous protest slogan from this era expresses, "We can't even get to the back of the bus."

By 1978, the regulations for the new law had still not been implemented by the Department of Health, Education, and Welfare (HEW), so its provisions were not being enforced across any federal agencies. To pressure the HEW secretary to sign the regulations, disabled people across the country held sit-in demonstrations at HEW offices that April. The longest sit-in lasted twenty-eight days in San Francisco, at the end of which the regulations were signed.[40]

These activists galvanized their fight for access to public life via a conscious shift from the way disability had been previously defined in the West—from the medical model to the social model of disability. The medical model is focused on fixing a disabled person, usually through modern medical means. Within this paradigm, a disability is a personal problem that the individual must cure through participation in the rehabilitative process (e.g., use of adaptive equipment, maximal mastery of daily-living skills, job training, etc.).[41]

In the social model, disability is viewed as merely another facet of human difference that becomes problematic only because the environment makes it so. Using a wheelchair is difficult not because someone cannot walk, but because most buildings have stairs. Remove the stairs; remove the problem. The same logic applies to audible crosswalks or access to closed-captioning for video content. When public space is accessible to the disability community, the disability itself loses salience. We can all be what we have always been—people with equal rights to participate in society.

THE ADA

The passing of the Americans with Disabilities Act in 1990 signaled a seminal victory for the social model. Building upon Section 504, the ADA extended accessibility mandates outside of federal funding channels to include all state and local government entities, as well as places of public accommodation (i.e., businesses). It also created a national telecommunication service for the Deaf, hard of hearing, and other communication-related disabilities. Imagine not having a guaranteed way to use the phone until this law passed. Although barriers remain for people with disabilities, the ADA cemented the accessibility conversation as a national priority.

As someone who inherited the benefits of the ADA and Section 504, I have humble respect for disability rights leaders like Judy Heumann and Justin Dart, Jr. Without their willingness to take the lead in mainstreaming accessibility, I would not have anything close to the access and services to which I am privileged. I would be living in a nursing home without a chance for education, employment, or participation in community life. I agree with the social model as an advocacy framework. It serves to humanize the disability experience. We are people with goals, dreams, and lives to enjoy. When the world is more accessible, we are able to enjoy it more completely. I support that outcome.

I do not buy the worldview claim that disability is normative, though. When I advocate for accessibility, I replace *normative* with *common*. Disability is a common, human experience. Because all people have God-given value, physical and social infrastructure should be responsive to these differences. Yet just because something is common does not make it part of ultimate reality, the way things were always meant to be. At this worldview juncture, I part ways with the social model while gratefully honoring its legacy of justifying equal rights for the disability community.

Despite increased accessibility, the social model remains a mostly in-group concept that failed to extend into society at large. Only people with disabilities and their families and friends tend to see disability as a product of mismatched environments. Societal stigma against disability remains. Laws cannot fix hearts. Stigma increases exponentially alongside the degree of a person's limitations, so broad access to social and civic life is still granted only to the most able. Alongside the social model of disability, another element of disability culture began to develop in hope it would provide a deeper solution to stigma.

DISABILITY AS AN IDENTITY

In *Demystifying Disability: What to Know, What to Say, and How to Be an Ally*, disability rights activist Emily Ladau provides a valuable touchpoint for the latest interpretation of disability. I recommend her book because she believes the worldview assumptions about disability similar to how most disabled adults believe today—disability is personal identity. While Ladau gives space for the social model and those within the disability community who do not emphasize disability identity, the thrust of her content both supports and is undergirded by disability identity. The identity model is interwoven into her definition of ultimate reality, which she shares in the following chapter opener:

> My relationship status with disability is complicated. On one hand, my disability is an integral facet of my being. It is completely intertwined with how I think and how I move. I consider it to be an identity—in many ways, my defining identity, although I don't want to be solely defined by it. Confusing, I know. I take pride in being disabled, and it's brought me to a whole culture and community that I love. But on the other hand, it's not always sunshine and roses. I struggle with physical pain every day. I feel the emotional toll from lack of acceptance, sometimes from others, sometimes within myself. But I am disabled. It's part of me.[42]

The identity model moves beyond acknowledging disability as a form of human difference to integrating it as a personal characteristic on the same plane as race and gender. Most disabled Americans ages forty and under likely ascribe to the identity model, and disability identity has been adapted into the larger milieu of intersecting social identities.

In graduate school, I lived alongside other students with physical disabilities, and I encountered the concept of disability identity for the first time. Until this point, it never occurred to me that disability could impact the identity of people, mine or others. I answer the deep questions of life differently than such social-identity metaphysics.

Since graduate school, I've been listening and attempting to build a context of understanding toward disability identity and its adjacent movement, disability pride. I've asked, "How did we get here?" and "Why is disability pride the accepted standard of justice?" I am not a scoffer toward ideas or people, even when I disagree. While all ideas are not equally true, each has reasons for existing. So how did we get here?

STIGMA

People with disabilities navigate a world constantly sending the message that there is something wrong with us. We are immediately *othered*. This *othering* produces a society in which disability becomes a larger-than-life factor encompassing and overshadowing our personhood. The overshadowing is stigma.

I learned a powerful lesson about stigma from a graduate school instructor. She challenged us to resist labeling people by their most visible or differing characteristic. That practice often communicates stigma. She told a story of attending a work meeting in which she pointed out an individual who another coworker wanted to meet.

She described the person by saying, "She's the woman in the pink shirt."

Upon hearing this description, the coworker said with slight irritation, "Why didn't you just say, 'The Black woman'?"

My instructor, herself an African American woman, used the story to teach that in a white-majority culture, people of color are often reduced to their skin color as an all-important factor of being.

The same reduction of being occurs with disability. I am "the girl in the wheelchair" before anything else. Most people do not even get to "woman." Those of us who use mobility devices are often reduced completely to those pieces of equipment in public. Transit operators and fellow elevator riders tell others to move because "a wheelchair is getting on." It is better to say "a wheelchair user." This simple addition protects personhood.

On a funny note, a bus driver accidentally drove past me one winter night. He stopped when I waved, and as I boarded, he said, "You're going to hate me for saying this, but I thought you were a trash bag." I laughed, taking responsibility for wearing an all-black coat and hood while sitting in an all-black wheelchair. I see how I might resemble a trash bag in the dark. I would rather be mistaken for a trash bag at night, though, than reduced to only my wheelchair in the daylight.

BECKY

When I was six years old, Grandma gave my sisters and I Barbie dolls for Christmas. Upon unwrapping mine, I found Becky. Becky was Mattel's attempt at disability inclusion. She was Barbie's wheelchair friend, complete with a manual wheelchair, service dog, and, to my dismay, flat feet to fit her tennis shoes. Anyone who's played with Barbie knows that 99 percent of all her shoes are universal because her feet are almost exclusively designed for high heels. Becky could not wear high heels. I later combed our local Toys "R" Us Barbie aisle in concentrated search of more interesting footwear opportunities for Becky. Perhaps I mimicked an internal quest for options in life, albeit on a miniature scale.

When I unwrapped Becky, I did not want her. I felt equally sad and guilty for not liking my present. I kept Becky, but I had a princess Barbie with a sparkling pink dress and pointed feet who was my doll of choice. My sisters and I shared our Barbies, and when we played with Becky, she was not often in her wheelchair. We never thought about it. Her wheelchair did not matter.

Children play imaginatively not to necessarily express who they are in the immediate, but to act out potentialities of who they may become. Grandma had good intentions when she bought me Becky. She thought it would help to have a doll with which I could identify. But Grandma miscalculated. I did not see myself as Becky, nor did I desire to become her. The sadness I felt in receiving the gift came from the beginning of an awareness that people would connect me with my wheelchair automatically as their primary response to my existence against my will.

Reducing someone to their disability is the cornerstone of stigma. We slowly erode the humanity and personhood of anyone we stigmatize. The less one can do or the more visible the disability, the more personhood is reduced and replaced by the presenting features of a diagnosis. Differences in ability become the defining characteristic used to evaluate acceptance and worth.

PITY AND PRAISE

In his monumental book *No Pity*, journalist Joseph Shapiro gives voice to what every disabled person intrinsically understands. The world fears us. To numb this fear response, Shapiro records how society resorts to two equally damaging stereotypes—one based on pity and the other on a twisted form of praise. "The Poster Child"[43] stereotype has been used as an advertising trope for medical research funding campaigns to elicit pity from an audience to generate donations. These involve pictures and videos of children with visible, physical conditions. Adults with disabilities are never featured in these campaigns because disability in adulthood is socially undesirable and will not evoke the same responses of pity necessary to motivate giving. The poster child stereotype reduces disabled people to objects of pity, subhuman recipients of alms given as a means to boost the givers' self-esteem.

The "supercrip"[44] (slang for *supercripple*) stereotype overemphasizes people with disabilities who experience success. It communicates that disabled people are only valuable via their capacity to achieve. The emphasis is on our performance and usefulness to the nondisabled world as objects of inspiration. Australian disability rights activist Stella Young popularized the term *inspiration porn*[45] to describe the problem of viewing people with disabilities exclusively as a source of inspiration. She called out the stereotype as objectifying and minimizing.

A risk in writing this book is I may be reduced to the "charismatic supercrip" whose sole purpose is to inspire the church. I'll pop that balloon in advance. I am a person intent on living a life worthy of the gospel. That is all. It is fine to be inspired by the Holy Spirit in my life; he inspires me daily. It is, however, stigmatizing to use inspiration language as a cover for surprise that the Holy Spirit flourishes in my life as fully as he can in anyone's life.

We can draw strength from one another without objectifying a person's disability. I worked for a Center for Independent Living (CIL), a nonprofit run by and for people with disabilities. One Monday morning, I was dragging my exhausted body through the workday. I left my office and rolled toward the receptionist's desk where a volunteer sat fielding calls. In between calls, he was reading a book in braille.

I stopped and asked, "What are you reading, Daryl?"

"The Bible," Daryl answered.

"What book?" I asked with piqued interest.

"Daniel," he said. "My church is going through the book, and I am trying to get caught up."

"What chapter?" I squeaked.

"Chapter 6."

"Chapter 6!" I repeated in delight. "I love chapter 6!"

"Oh yeah," Daryl replied. "It's a good one."

Daryl continued reading, and I rolled back to my office with a hopeful heart. Daniel 6 is the lion's den story. It shares the truth of a faithful God who protects those who serve him. I sat at my desk for a moment, whispering a quiet thank you to God for encouraging my heart through Daryl. He was just living his life, reading the Bible, but he returned my gaze to the Father's face. I drew strength from my brother that day. This type of inspiration is okay. The heart posture to avoid would be me saying to Daryl, "Wow, it inspires me that you read the Bible even though you're blind." His blindness does not inspire me.

In philosophical terms, the inspiration stereotype is an ethical argument based on utility (i.e., usefulness) masqueraded in the language of respect. It communicates that people with disabilities should only be included in society because we serve an inspiring purpose to the nondisabled world. What happens if we lose strength and become too weak and limited to inspire anymore? Do we lose access to love, respect, and dignity?

Often, the answer is yes. This is why disabled people with significant needs are still marginalized in society or much worse.

Someone told me once, "If I was in your situation, I would

pull the plug." This person thought she made a statement about herself, but she made a value judgment upon my life. Sadly, this is not the only time similar vile words have been said to my face. I'll never get used to it; it will never be okay. These words reveal a narrative that permeates our world, albeit often in disguise—disabled lives have less value.

CHAPTER 5

The Eugenics Fallout (Disability Culture Part 2)

The world's dismay over disability manifests at its worst in the systematic destruction of life. Once you can no longer be considered cute and worthy of pity or a successful source of inspiration, the world system has no use for you. We should not separate the origins of the disability identity worldview from a humble, sensitive awareness of the eugenics movement in the West.

The eugenics movement gained traction in Western cultural dialogue at the turn of the twentieth century. Relying on the ideological foundation of the Darwinian notion "survival of the fittest," *eugenics* is the attempt to produce the most desirable population by eliminating those deemed unfit.[46] People with disabilities have always been placed in the unfit category.

The most flagrant example of eugenics is the murder of an estimated 250,000 adults and children with disabilities under the Nazi T4 program. Some died by lethal injection. Some starved to death; some were gassed. T4 was the test run of the model that would be used shortly after to murder six million Jewish people in death camps like Auschwitz.[47] Once we draw an arbitrary line determining which lives have value, we lose any claim to an objective standard that would prevent further carnage.

Although the Third Reich has ended, bioethical concerns surrounding eugenics are far from solved. The ideological exchanges between eugenics, genetic testing, and the abortion conversation in the West are intensified for disabled people. Some European nations claim to have nearly eradicated Down syndrome, meaning that after babies in the womb show positive genetic tests for Down syndrome and other genetic conditions, they are routinely and systematically aborted.[48]

Advocates with Down syndrome and their families rightly question the ethical standards of countries that celebrate the elimination of human life based on genetic differences. Consider this comment from a New Zealand health administrator Michael Laws on his frustrations with advocacy against genetic testing.

> I think most women, having discovered they're carrying a Downs Syndrome fetus, would abort. Dear Lord, very natural reaction. Incredibly though there are a group of DS activists (the parents of)

The Eugenics Fallout (Disability Culture Part 2) | 89

who want to DENY this test to expectant mothers because they think it has the potential to eradicate Downs Syndrome. And I'm thinking: what a bloody fantastic achievement that would be. Next: multiple sclerosis.[49]

His words ooze with a eugenics mindset. Again, as this quote hints at, once we draw a line designating which lives are most valuable, how do we prevent that line from adjusting infinitely?

WHO GETS TO LIVE?

Alongside abortion, concerns regarding physician-assisted suicide remain a high priority among the disability community. In *No Pity*, Shapiro records a harrowing story about a hospitalized man with paralysis whose suicide ideation went unquestioned by doctors and judges. His life was saved only by the intervention of friends who helped him pursue his options toward independent living outside of the hospital or a nursing home. Shapiro accurately comments, "a nondisabled man who asked the state to help him end his life would get suicide-prevention counseling, but McAfee had not been considered rash or even depressed. Instead, a judge had praised him as sensible and brave."[50]

The National Council on Disability (NCD) published a five-part report on disability and bioethics in 2019. The report addresses how policies such as physician-assisted suicide, genetic testing, transplant protocols, and quality-of-life metrics in the insurance industry reinforce the social undesirability of disability. This undesirability leads to abuse and discrimination. In part 4 of the report, *Genetic Testing and the Race to Perfection*, the NCD summarizes the problem:

> The distinction between "perfectly normal" and "broken" is not an objective medical bright line in the sand, but a normative judgment that reflects human prejudice, disability stereotypes, and the social and physical barriers that place arbitrary limits on the length and quality of life of people with many disabilities.[51]

In the world, there is no line between "your body is broken" and "you are broken."

During the onset of the COVID-19 pandemic, it shocked me how much advocacy occurred at a state and national level to protect against care-rationing provisions that discriminated against people with disabilities. The question of who gets the ventilator when there is a shortage—the twenty-year-old man with no disabilities or the thirty-five-year-old man with Down syndrome—and the basis on which that decision is made is problematic. But I can predict the standard answer. If there is a shortage of ventilators, or even a fear of such a shortage, disabled people may not get them. Instead, we expect pressure to sign a do-not-resuscitate order, even when our diagnoses are not terminal. I am not overdramatizing. This is real. The world system is not designed to protect life. The disability community lives in full view of this vulnerability.

Disability identity is how many disabled people have chosen to thrive in the face of unrelenting stigma. It makes sense that a group of people told all their lives that they have no value should choose to believe the opposite about themselves. The goal of the disability identity worldview is to take power away from stigma by embracing what society denigrates. I would never despise anyone for making that choice. I do not see another option in a postmodern, naturalistic world. If we are only our bodies and brains plus the composite of our social identities, disability identity may be the best choice.

DEFRAUDING PAIN

But I will not pretend that such a choice produces life. I've never seen any disabled person who lives every moment according to the belief system of disability identity. This is because it defrauds us of the reality of pain. We can talk a good game, but the grief of disability is real. Disability identity does no justice to the hard, intractable limits we face. We find this tension in Emily Ladau's quote I introduced earlier.

We all want to "make it." We want what all human beings want, and we grieve when we cannot make developmental or societal milestones for whatever reason. I see this grief and struggle seeping through the cracks in the identity worldview. It drips through conversations with friends, social media posts, and advocacy meetings. The slow trickle only widens the crack, and eventually, we find a gushing stream of pain behind the plaster of disability identity. Superimposing disability onto ourselves is not a solution to the discord in our lives.

A disabled friend recently came to me expressing she felt like "a bad person" for not embracing disability pride. She said, "I just don't feel that way." I told her the truth that disability was not her identity and explained she was not morally compromised for disagreeing with that ideology. She does not have to make her body's loss part of who she is in order to be loved.

This is the option given to disabled people in the West. We are supposed to become the suffering we experience as a protection against the world's continual minimization of our existence. When any of us suggests there is a different answer to the problem of suffering on the earth than social identity metaphysics offers, we are labeled ableist traitors. Yet even these angry labels are merely masks for pain.

Many disabled people remain fundamentally opposed to the idea of healing because if healing is possible within the universe, then disability is demonstrably not connected to a person's being. As soon as that domino falls, disability identity loses its salience as a means to survive the real trauma of the world's rejection. It is easier to simply close the worldview door on any reversal of circumstances. When charismatic Christians knock on this door, we must knock gently.

DISABILITY STRENGTHS

Before the pendulum swings too far in the grief direction, I will balance it. The disability community does not spend each day in gloom or despair over our circumstances. While there is legitimate loss, we do not perceive our existence as tragic. We are people with lives to embrace. Although the identity model breaks apart as soon as we make an authentic seat at the table for pain, the majority of us live happily. Pain is part of being human. Our lives are worth living.

A common argument used to bolster the disability identity worldview is to emphasize the positive aspects of disability. Like with the social model, I agree with the baseline principle—disability has its plus sides. Many Autistic people are highly creative and offer needed talents that enrich our world. People with mobility disabilities are the original life hackers. We were doing it long before it was cool on TikTok, and we still are coming up with ingenious ways to "do life." The Deaf have a separate language and culture, and many of them prefer being deaf because of this cultural-linguistic heritage. We should respect all these strengths, and I do. While everyone can hear in heaven, God will receive worship eternally in sign language. He is worthy of adoration and love expressed in all languages.

I played Paralympic boccia for fifteen years, and I enjoyed competing at the national and international elite level. Boccia was a coed sport during the years I played, and I took no small pleasure in winning against male athletes twice my age and size.

Although I lost my share of games, all my boccia friends knew I was a challenge to beat. Paralympic sport taught me how to work toward goals, develop competence over time, and solve problems. Even though I was playing against disabled people, I never thought about disability while competing. It was not the focus. We were just people playing because we loved the game, and we were good at it. I treasure my boccia experience and the positive elements it brought into my life.

The existence of positive facets to disability, however, is still not a one-to-one correlation that disability and identity are equivalent. That logic does not make sense. Just because we have experienced something does not mean we become it. This conflation of identity and experience is one of the deepest lies of our time. The concept is born from the Herculean effort required to stabilize personal worth in a relativistic culture where there are no absolute standards anymore.

SELF-FIRST WORLDVIEWS

The disability identity worldview is as an attempt to create a human-centered solution for rejection and pain. There simply is no such solution. Under this worldview, identity seems to be the sum of our characteristics and experiences arranged and prioritized with the *self* as the sole arbiter. Starting with the self as the standard of reality, these ideas morph philosophy and theology around the self's various identities, rather than allowing God to define who we are and build our lives from his definition.

Worldview structures based ultimately on the self can never

produce life in themselves. They lead to relativism, which is the everyone-has-their-own-truth doctrine. There are no logical or otherwise compelling reasons to concede worldview ground to relativism and its only possible consequence—the absolute wilderness of nihilism. Truth exists, and the self is not its definer.

Ultimate reality is deeper than our experiences. If we agree a person's identity is not based upon differences in ability, we are empowered to love and protect the dignity of all people as well as to recognize the existence of loss. We escape the false shame-pride dichotomy. There is truly nothing "wrong" with people who have cerebral palsy or low vision because their identity and value do not change. But cerebral palsy and low vision cause tangible, legitimate loss.

Despite reasons for questioning the validity of disability identity, I am in the minority among Western disabled people. If they read this book, they may view me as a sellout who has broken faith with disability culture. I am a sellout. I sold out to the crucified and resurrected Messiah long ago.

Emily Ladau is Jewish, so we differ theologically from the outset. I have no expectation we would be on the same page when it comes to supernatural healing. She did not give space in her book to any connection between her faith and disability. I would genuinely love to learn her approach to Scriptures like Isaiah 35:5–6 and Zephaniah 3:19. The first one addresses physical healing, and the second one touches on reversal of stigma. They are beautiful promises. But again, I have no expectation of agreement.

HEALING IS NOT EUGENICS

Between the first and final draft of this book, scholar and Shakespeare lecturer Amy Kenny published *My Body Is Not a Prayer Request: Disability Justice in the Church*, the Christian companion piece to Ladau's book. There were moments of agreement. We share a passion for church accessibility and obeying Luke 14. I groaned as she told a horrific story about someone shaming her for not accepting healing prayer. I winced in understanding of the pain when charismatic Christians equate her nerve spasms to "demonic convulsions."[52] She gave a compelling interpretation of Jacob's hip-wrenching episode when he wrestled with God as the turning point in his character transformation (although I'm not sure that the injury outweighs the face-to-face encounter Israel experienced with God as the true catalyst).

Although there is not space to address all of Kenny's arguments here (see more on my website blog[53]), her comments about physical healing merit a response.

Like all self-first logic, Kenny begins with disability identity as ultimate and then organizes her theology around that construct. As such, there was little room for a miracle-working God in her discussion of disability and Christianity. Kenny screams against Christians who believe in supernatural healing, calling us "prayerful perpetrators."[54] She labels physical healing "benevolent eugenics"[55] and parallels healing prayer to "a magic trick."[56] Those are dark words. Kenny promotes the worldview claim that Christians who believe in healing commit acts of discrimination by even suggesting healing disability is good. Kenny has the freedom in Jesus to decide healing is not meaningful to her, but it is not sinful to celebrate God's healing gifts or discrimination to consider them good. I am not offended by Kenny; I understand and empathize with how she reached her conclusions. I am livid at the snake, though. I despise him and his lies against the Holy One of Israel.

No, Jesus's healing power is not any form of eugenics. Jesus has been healing disability centuries before eugenics developed. Eugenics arose from evolutionary theory that Satan applies to bring destruction and death on the earth. God does not destroy life when he heals; he renews life. The difference is night and day. But the devil would love nothing more than for the disability community to associate Jesus's good works with Satan's own vile practices. He's been calling the gift of tongues evil since the first Pentecost. It sounds just like his putrid heart to foster similar deception toward gifts of healing. I reject his redefinition of good and evil.

Kenny attempts to rescue Jesus from becoming chief among the prayerful perpetrators by driving a wedge between *curing* and *healing* in John 9. Kenny says the healed man, who she names Zach, was kicked out of the synagogue because the leaders were motivated by stigma against his past blindness. She narrates,

> He might be cured, but he is cast out of the community that should bring healing. Curing his blindness doesn't change the social aspects of his disability:

> exclusion from worship inside the temple, inaccurate perceptions of his sin, and segregation from the broader community. The neighbors still think he was "born entirely in sins" even after Zach is given sight (9:34). True healing would remedy those social aspects of disability instead of abandoning him in social isolation. Healing would remove the stigma of his disability rather than focusing on its physical aspects.[57]

Yes, the religious leaders malign Zach, saying, "You were steeped in sin at birth" (John 9:34), communicating their faulty judgment that his previous disability resulted from sin. But he was not kicked out of the community because of stigma against that past condition. He was rejected because he believed Jesus came from God. That's why the community leaders expel Zach.[58] If he had renounced Jesus's divinely authorized healing power, or at least feigned ignorance like his parents had, Zach would not have been shown the door.

The conversation between Jesus and him at the end of the narrative contains a deep, largely untapped reservoir of Jesus's beauty. Yet their dialogue accentuates, not minimizes, the man's healed sight (see chapter 12). Kenny writes, "There are no magic pills, quick fixes, or wish-granting genies when it comes to holistic healing. There's Jesus, who wants to be with us: Emmanuel."[59] Yes, and Emmanuel overflows with majesty to heal the earth. Jesus masterfully brings deep healing to each person he touches.

Yet, his majestically good healing power never denigrates physical restoration to second-rate goodness.

OFFENSE IS A MISSED OPPORTUNITY

The above words will not reach Amy Kenny. They do not touch her pain. She says, "I wish prayerful perpetrators were free from the lie that I am worth less because my body works differently."[60] Ah, there's the wound.

What should I do? I'm the hateful prayerful perpetrator. The one who supposedly spits upon Kenny's value by denying disability is anyone's identity. I'm the backward charismatic who needs to repent of my internalized ableism. I'm the one, she believes, who holds her life in contempt.

Do I pass by my sister as she bleeds from stigma's assault on the roadside? If I come close, should I rip her wounds open with my theology? I have the knowledge to discredit the disability identity worldview from the Scripture, but of what use is my knowledge if I cannot reach my sister's heart.

I could match scream for scream when Kenny says I am filled with prejudice for believing Jesus put all his skin in the game to heal disability. Or I could humble myself and join my beloved Lord, who has no problem coming low enough to wash her feet.

While washing, I would say to her, "My holy sister, I'm sorry charismatic Christians have left your heart so black-and-blue. We do not agree, but I hear you. I see your pain. Don't you know, my sister, that you no longer have to fight for your value? You can breathe now. Jesus has no plans to hurt you. No plans to shame you or force his power on you. Jesus treasures you now, and I promise his healing touch never cancels your worth."

Rather than silencing the disability community, we can connect to the pain behind disability identity—the longing to be deeply seen, heard, known, and wanted. The desire to be chosen. Instead of arguing, I would rather use the truth to see if I can come low enough to showcase afresh the heartbeat of God.

After reading *My Body Is Not a Prayer Request*, I realized the worldview crossfire was more intense than I'd ever imagined. So I tried to surpass it with the intensity of God's goodness. I filled in additional specifics of my relationship with God in chapters 1 and 3 out of a burdened desire to magnify God's excellent heart accessed through his supernatural gifts and presence. The nicknames, the snuggles, the delight, and the healing are available when we come close. It's our covenant inheritance.

Our covenant God comes low to lovingly redeem us from our limiting ideas into a glorious definition of being that offers eternal value and a secure, steadfast identity. I will come low with him. Some people may accept the invitation; others may not. Regardless, I want people like Amy Kenny and Emily Ladau to experience that the God I represent is a father, lover, friend, and a faithful deliverer.

CHAPTER 6

The Exodus God

I left Emily Ladau's worldview house seeking an alternative. I knew a scholar published a two-volume anthology of documented miracles. When I googled something like "documented evidence for miracles," I found Dr. Keener's newest book, *Miracles Today* (introduced in chapter 3), a reader-friendly follow-up to his massive academic anthology. Ladau and Keener published their books forty-two days apart in the fall of 2021, and I read them on the same day (though not all of Keener's). In his book, Keener compiled extensive records of healings across the globe. He's talked with people who had quadriplegia who are walking today, people with blindness who are seeing, people who were deaf who can now hear every word of this book if they read it aloud.

Transitioning between books felt like I left a monochromatic universe and re-entered a cosmos containing the full, colorful spectrum of light. Keener and I construct our worldview houses similarly. We believe God loves all people and he has provided a way in Jesus for humanity to be restored to our original design as spiritual reflectors of God's image. We also believe God is reconciling, and will one day fully restore, all of his physical creation to its original design without any decay, pain, or loss.

This restoration is the exclusive starting point for justice; there is no true justice apart from the righteous King of all the earth. As we wait for the fullness of his promises, God uses his power to confirm the truth of restoration in Jesus and to show us some of the final justice that is on its way. These demonstrations include medically verified healings of disability. Take Marlene for example.

MARLENE

As I skimmed Keener's table of contents, I quickly turned to the story of a woman named Marlene who Jesus healed of cerebral palsy. That's my diagnosis, and I'd never read a record of healing for this condition. Keener personally interviewed Marlene. He describes Marlene's intimate relationship with the Holy Spirit and her journey into the recognition that God wanted to heal her body. Keener writes,

> Marlene became a committed Christian at age eleven, when some Christians in her high school, one of whom had specifically felt led to reach out to her,

> invited her to a Youth for Christ meeting.... Soon after her conversion, she began to pray with words she did not understand, because at such times she experienced feelings of God embracing her. She was as yet unaware of any biblical term for this.[61]

Keener continues,

> Marlene took for granted that cerebral palsy was God's plan for her life and remained content. In the years that followed, however, she began to question this assumption, as her condition became increasingly severe. She lost much of her eyesight and became effectively paralyzed from the neck down. Some of her muscle spasms were so severe that her seizures had broken the bones of those trying to care for her.... When she was seventeen, she began to question whether this condition itself was God's ideal plan for her.[62]

There are different types of cerebral palsy, and I do not have the type that causes involuntary movement strong enough to break a bone. But I understand all too well what muscle spasms feel like. I could never read the description of what was happening to Marlene's body and write it off as a part of her identity or merely another aspect of human difference. She was hurting. The pain is what is wrong, not Marlene herself.

Keener shares how God gave Marlene a vision of receiving healing at a church on an exact day: March 29. When that day came, Marlene asked the Lord to help her contact the right church. She directed a nurse to open the yellow pages to local churches, and the Holy Spirit showed her the church she was supposed to call. The nurse helped Marlene contact the pastor who, after some persuasion, took her to his church. As the congregation prayed, God healed Marlene. Her legs and feet straightened, and after walking several laps around the sanctuary perimeter with assistance, Marlene could walk, speak, and move without restriction. God also fully restored her vision to better than twenty-twenty sight. Her doctors at the Mayo Clinic were shocked by the reversal of her condition, and they verified the healing with diagnostic tests.[63]

COLLISION

The worldviews of disability culture and charismatic Christianity are now on track for a headlong collision. I part company with the disability community on the identity idea because identities do not come from external or internal differences. I also believe God ultimately has better plans for our lives than pain. Disability will always be common until Jesus comes back, but disability itself is not the endgame of existence, nor does it have to be the endpoint of anyone's story.

Equally so, disability does not make people inherently "broken." While I have a body with significant limits, I am not broken.

Because of Jesus, I am inherently whole already, a concept that I will unpack in the next chapter. Healing does not compromise the worth of disabled people. All are made in the image of God—designed for deep, tender relationships with him and one another.

Every worldview has an ultimate story, a metanarrative, that people use to make sense of and access the world around them. The Christian metanarrative is the record of God's interaction with his creation found in the Bible. For us to demonstrate the heart of God to the disability community, we must model our response from God's own breathtaking, luminous activity in his world. I want to take us back to one of the earliest stories in that big story.

The exodus of Israel from Egypt is an epic identity reset narrative. It chronicles how God rescues his people from an oppressive regime and faithfully journeys with them as they transition from national, generational slaves to become a redeemed, covenanted people in which the presence of God tangibly dwells. Talk about a reversal of circumstances. Let's set the stage, shall we?

THE GOD WHO KNOWS

In Genesis 15, God makes and self-fulfills a covenant (i.e., a binding legal agreement between parties) with a man named Abram, whom God later renames Abraham. As part of this covenant, God promises that Abram will have a son and, through this son, will have many descendants. God also promises these descendants the land of Canaan. But God explains that there will be suffering before Abram's descendants take possession of this land. He reinforces to Abram,

> Know for certain that for four hundred years your descendants will be strangers in a country not their own and that they will be enslaved and mistreated there. But I will punish the nation they serve as slaves, and afterward they will come out with great possessions. (Gen. 15:13–14)

The circumstances of Abraham's family occurred just as God said. Jacob, Abraham's grandson, travels to Egypt with all his family to escape famine, and they live there.

The exodus account begins after the four hundred years God identified to Abraham. His descendants have multiplied and now compose a large nation. Their numbers intimidate the Egyptians, who conscript them into forced labor so they do not join Egypt's enemies and fight against them. In the midst of this suffering, God saves the life of a baby named Moses, who is rescued from Pharaoh's command that all the Israelite baby boys be drowned in the Nile. Moses grows up in Pharaoh's house and lives in Egypt until he murders an Egyptian overseer in an attempt to assist his fellow Israelites. This act forces Moses to flee into the wilderness to escape Pharaoh's wrath.

At this less-than-ideal moment, the narrator provides a summary on which the rest of the book, and the whole biblical story, hinges.

> During those many days the king of Egypt died, and the people of Israel groaned because of their slavery and cried out for help. Their cry for rescue from slavery came up to God. And God *heard* their groaning, and God *remembered* his covenant with Abraham, with Isaac, and with Jacob. God *saw* the people of Israel—and God *knew*. (Ex. 2:23–25 ESV, emphasis added)

In this summary, we catch a glimpse into the character of God. He responds to a cry. He hears this intense groaning and remembers his covenant with Israel. Theologian Victor Hamilton describes,

> The God of v. 24 is a God who hears and remembers. How could anybody cry out from pain (to whomever), and God not hear? How could God be God and be oblivious to such wailing? Does recalling that Hebrew šāma' means not only "hear" but also "obey" suggest that for God not to hear is for God not to obey, as strange as that might sound?

God remembering his covenant does not mean that the cries of the Israelites jog his forgetful memory. Hamilton notes that "remembering" expresses God taking "deliberate action on what is recalled."[64] God is relationally attentive and responsive to his people.

The weighty theme of God's responsive heart carries through

the rest of the story. When God calls Moses to be his tool of deliverance, he contextualizes the calling first by personalizing the same truths.

> The LORD said, "I have indeed seen the misery of my people in Egypt. I have heard them crying out because of their slave drivers, and I am concerned about their suffering. So I have come down to rescue them from the hand of the Egyptians and to bring them up out of that land into a good and spacious land, a land flowing with milk and honey—the home of the Canaanites, Hittites, Amorites, Perizzites, Hivites and Jebusites." (Ex. 3:7–8)

Hamilton emphasizes that "God's saving/delivering work is both a saving 'from' and a saving 'to,' a deliverance from bondage and an old way of life, and entry into freedom and a revolutionary new way of life."[65]

Just as the Israelite community experienced unilateral stigma, defined by their slavery status in Egypt, so too does the world reduce the disability community to our physiological differences. Forget dreams, desires, and hopes. Forget personhood and relational connection. We become the wheelchair friend, the blind student, the Down syndrome employee. If stigma does anything well, it makes us invisible. Many of us are simply accustomed to this dynamic. We do not anticipate respect. We face into being ignored, minimized, and misunderstood. No matter how hard we try to prove ourselves, we can never outwork or outperform the stigma of disability.

Although we do not perceive disability itself as tragic, we still need to know God takes notice and cares about every second of pain, every demeaning word and action, and each tear of acknowledged or unacknowledged grief. Whether we have a relationship with God, we are crying out in our own ways, and there is a longing in all of us to experientially discover somebody is moving toward us, not away from us. We crave to be seen, heard, and known. How we need the Exodus God to remove our invisibility and heal stigma's sting.

THE GOD WHO FULFILLS HIS COVENANT

When God sends Moses back to Egypt, Moses and Aaron tell the Israelite elders that God is going to deliver the nation, and they perform the confirming signs that God gave Moses. The initial response of the Israelites to the signs and the promise is one of expectation and hope. Exodus 4:31 tells us, "And when they heard that the LORD was concerned about them and had seen their misery, they bowed down and worshiped." Notice even here that the hope is connected to the demonstrated truth that God attends to their suffering and has personally come to them.

It would be nice to say everything goes smoothly from there, but circumstances go from bad to desperate. Moses and Aaron come before Pharaoh for the first time, and the result of that conversation is the Israelites' work becomes harder. Pharaoh orders Israel to be given no more straw to make bricks, but the people are mandated to continue making the same number of bricks per day. In modern terms, this would be something like an already intense twelve-hour workday becoming an eighteen-hour workday. The Israelite overseers go to Pharaoh and ask for a reprieve. He doubles down against them, insisting they are lazy. He will work them harder so that they ignore the deliverance promises God is making through Moses. In response, the Israelite community is understandably angry with Moses and Aaron. Moses complains to God.[66]

God ignores Moses's frustration and uses this moment to reinforce his character and covenant-based promises to Israel. In the reinforcement, God initiates a shift in the way he is to be known by the Israelites. He declares his unique, covenantal name.

> God also said to Moses, "I am the LORD. I appeared to Abraham, to Isaac and to Jacob as God Almighty, but by my name the LORD I did not make myself fully known to them. I also established my covenant with them to give them the land of Canaan, where they resided as foreigners. Moreover, I have heard the groaning of the Israelites, whom the Egyptians are enslaving, and I have remembered my covenant.
>
> "Therefore, say to the Israelites: 'I am the LORD, and I will bring you out from under the yoke of the Egyptians. I will free you from being slaves to them, and I will redeem you with an outstretched arm and

with mighty acts of judgment. I will take you as my own people, and I will be your God. Then you will know that I am the LORD your God, who brought you out from under the yoke of the Egyptians. And I will bring you to the land I swore with uplifted hand to give to Abraham, to Isaac and to Jacob. I will give it to you as a possession. I am the LORD.'" (Ex. 6:2–8)

Hamilton suggests we interpret this moment as a shift in God's relationship with his people uniquely demonstrated to them through the events of the exodus. Hamilton explains,

> A knowledge of God as LORD/YHWH will emerge from the experience of these events that would be impossible without the experience of these events, even if one were cognizant of the vocable Y-H-W-H.[67]

The point of this name revelation is not ultimately about knowing God's name but about having a tangible experience of God's covenantal nature as expressed in his redeeming, rescuing power. Through the events of the exodus, God will showcase his name and nature to separate Israel from Egypt and the nations, wooing them into a unique, God-and-humanity covenant relationship. Hamilton underscores the beauty of the statement "I will take you as my own people" in chapter 6 verse 7: "The

Hebrew reads, literally, 'I will take you to me/myself (lî) as a people.' . . . Before God desires to bring Israel to Canaan, he desires to bring Israel to himself."[68]

There is enough tender desire in the above offer that we should weep. Not only does God dramatically free Israel from their suffering, but they are also beckoned into covenantal intimacy with him as the catalyst for inheriting the promised land. What a precious, powerful invitation. As Hamilton aptly summarizes, "Fellowship and intimacy trump relocation."[69]

But the Israelites do not respond to these encouraging words. Exodus 6:9 records, "Moses reported this to the Israelites, but they did not listen to him because of their discouragement and harsh labor." God rebukes the Israelites for their refusal to listen and for their lack of faith, right? No, at this point God simply continues with his plan.[70] The next nine chapters of Exodus detail how God proves himself to Israel and Egypt by rescuing the Israelites from Pharaoh through repeated acts of his power. When God takes Israel to himself in covenant at Mount Sinai, he will ask for their faithful obedience. But God first gives them time to experience who he is before requiring their surrendered trust.

USING OUR WORDS

Some of you may be thinking, *Okay, we need to ignore the protests of the disability community against healing and pray for them anyway so we can demonstrate God's power to rescue them.* Nope, not at all. We must allow God to continue with his plan, and not let our agendas get in the way. God's demonstrations of power in Exodus do showcase his nature, but those power displays are anchored to a specific purpose.

He is moving in power to shepherd Israel away from the mindset of being Egypt's slaves and into becoming the covenanted, treasured possession of the one true God. He commands Moses to speak this over Israel multiple times before he does any tangible delivering, and Moses follows God's lead.[71] God also uses a multi-sign approach to accomplish this goal. He could have accomplished the exodus in one fell swoop.[72] Instead, he tactfully chose repetitive demonstrations of power that functioned as object lessons for Israel of their covenant position before God—a display so convincing that many Egyptians likewise choose to follow Israel's God and accompany Israel as they leave Egypt.[73] Tactful, intentional power is the deliverance pathway to reset the identity of a people group.

It is the same with the disability community today. Even though Spirit-filled believers think healing is great, healing prayer is not the way in the door to their identity reset system. There are powerful truths to communicate and gifts of the Spirit to share that are more useful in opening a closed worldview door. God's heartbeat for people never changes. He was intentional and specific toward Israel when he rescued them. He will also be intentional and specific toward people with disabilities.

Rather than a one-size-fits-all healing power program, what would it look like for the charismatic church to take a page from God's exodus story and first speak relational identity, covenant-based belonging, and divine purpose into the lives of the disability community? Like God's proclamation to Israel, we need to bookend any faith for circumstantial change between the declaration of who God is, who people are, and his promise of covenantal relationship. We also must follow the Lord's leading and not run ahead based on our perceptions. Besides healing, God has other equally beautiful intentions, and intimacy still supersedes the reversal of circumstances every time.

We find these Exodus themes in Marlene's testimony. First, a Christian saw her as a person God loves and invited her to learn about the relationship into which God pursued her. Second, Marlene tangibly experienced a relationship with God. Among his other comforts, he gave her the gift of tongues before she had the language to define it. Third, from the context of their relationship, Marlene allowed the Holy Spirit to change her perspective on disability so that she could open to the possibility of supernatural healing.

Before the disability community can open their worldview to the concept of healing, they will likewise need to hear the love song of the passionate, pursuing God who wants to take them to himself. Unlike the stigmatizing world system, they need to know God is not disgusted by their limitations or weakness. He is not impatiently waiting for them to catch up or change. As they are now, he is not ashamed to call them his people. It is only in this knowledge that hope for any other promises matures. Without it, the Spirit-filled church's healing emphasis will be experienced like the obnoxious, laborious burden of making bricks without straw.

BRICKS WITHOUT STRAW

It is never appropriate to pray for healing of disability without the person's consent. This happens frequently because nondisabled people assume they can take charge of the personal decisions of disabled people. The resulting pain from such encounters can be lasting. Emily Ladau describes how she felt after a child prayed for her healing without permission. She had been preparing for a job interview, and she records,

> I felt like a deflated balloon. There I was, preparing for a big moment, mustering all the confidence I had, only to be snapped out of it with a reminder that people believe my body is a mistake, my existence is wrong . . . I still wish I could find that girl and her mother to take back the thank-you I gave them, to let them know that in spite of the religious model lens through which they viewed my disability, I'm not broken and I don't need prayers to be fixed.[74]

Sit with that quote for a moment. Can you see why she felt like they viewed her as a mistake, even if that messaging was unintended? Can you see how she interpreted this moment as stigma against disability? Did she encounter God's perspective *of her* or merely a human reaction *to her*?

A child inappropriately praying for healing is as benign as it gets in charismatic circles. If that broke this woman's confidence, consider the manifold damage if somebody had rebuked *a spirit of infirmity* or prayed against generational curses in her bloodline. The situation could have been far worse than a child not guided into good boundaries.

Here is the bottom line. God would not have left this daughter feeling like her existence was wrong. He would have approached her holistically and would certainly not have forced his healing power on her. Wouldn't it have been far better if the mother-daughter pair had gotten a word of knowledge about the interview to encourage her? Wouldn't it have been beautiful if they had spoken value into her life? She would have left the room full, not empty. Seen, not erased. God's treasure, not a mistake.

TRUTH AND HUMILITY

If someone responds to our offer of healing prayer with "No, my disability is a part of who I am. It's my identity," the last thing to do is slam the person with a counterargument. Saying arrogantly, "Well, you're wrong" will communicate to the disability community that we are following the course of the world and its long history of ignoring them. Hearts will seal shut.

Truth and humility are mutually reinforcing, not mutually

exclusive. When we encounter disability identity, we can ask these types of questions to build a bridge between God's heart and people:

- What does identity mean to you?
- Where does identity come from?
- What's your story of self-accepting your disability?
- What do you long for or value most?

These questions require we take our time to love people rather than pushing our perspective because we want to see our preferred outcome. Jesus always had time for people. He is an excellent bridge-builder into hearts, and so is the Holy Spirit. Neither builds bridges at random though. The Exodus God always moves with intentionality and purpose, to call people into covenant with himself.

I am not suggesting we stop praying for healing. I am exhorting us to stop making healing of disability the ultimate sign and wonder and instead to use everything the Holy Spirit has given to demonstrate God's heart. We should attend to the principles of the exodus as we interact with disabled people. Follow God's specific directions, speak covenant truth into people's hearts, and obediently use all the signs God has made available to us. Healing is not a replacement for doing the work of an evangelist,[75] allowing the Holy Spirit to construct his heart bridges as he sees fit.

"ESPECIALLY PROPHECY"

Prophecy is much more likely to impact the hearts of disabled people than healing. Prophecy communicates that God made us, knows us intricately, and calls us into an identity and destiny in his family. Words of knowledge are the kingdom's antidote to stigma and its erasure of personhood. And just like healing, prophecy has power to confirm the gospel.

Paul counsels the Corinthian church to "follow the way of love and eagerly desire gifts of the Spirit, especially prophecy" (1 Cor. 14:1). Prophecy is to be prioritized because it brings conviction and lifts people into their God-given purpose. Paul explains, "The one who prophesies speaks to people for their strengthening, encouraging and comfort" (1 Cor. 14:3). A few sentences later, Paul further endorses the power of prophecy:

> But if an unbeliever or an inquirer comes in while everyone is prophesying, they are convicted of sin and are brought under judgment by all, as the secrets of their hearts are laid bare. So they will fall down and worship God, exclaiming, "God is really among you!" (1 Cor. 14:24–25)

The context of this text is comparing and contrasting the benefits of prophecy and the gift of tongues to Christians and non-Christians. At this moment in culture, offers of healing prayer sound like a strange language to the disability community, causing non-Christians, and often Christians, to leave our gatherings in underwhelmed confusion. We think we are doing them a great service, but they only encounter more stigma and are thus shortchanged from meeting the God who knows them and calls them to himself. One Holy Spirit–empowered statement communicating the invitation to covenant with God is more valuable than a thousand prayers for healing.

The gift of knowing who God is and who I am before his face strengthens my heart like nothing else. It does not matter now how much the world's stigma seeks to shatter my value. I know who I am, and I have confidence in my God. I have entered his promised rest, and he will make his name and heart known through my life.

ABBA'S VOICE

I once told the Father, "I fit nowhere!" Most charismatics don't know how to respond to my disability, and most disabled people think I'm "out to lunch" for believing healing is a legitimate, good possibility. I seem to fit nowhere.

You fit pretty well between my shoulders, the Father answered, obviously echoing Deuteronomy 33:12.

I love every gift in supernatural Christianity, but there is none so valuable as hearing Abba's voice. I'm with Moses and Jesus, I need that gift to live.[76] According to my Father's voice, I do not become the stigma others attach to my existence, nor do I become the limitation in my body as a boomeranging reflex against that stigma. I am his daughter, born anew of his Spirit, free to not respond to the world's hollow descriptions of me in any form.

As the charismatic church proactively shares the gospel with the disability community while speaking Abba's heart through the prophetic gifts, we will see a generation of people rise who are unshackled from the world's definitions of their lives, ready to take unprecedented worldview territory and reclaim it for God's covenant purposes. This can only happen to the extent that charismatic believers allow our eyes to be directed to God's three-dimensional perspective of people.

CHAPTER 7

The Dignity of Three-Dimensional Existence

When I was first diagnosed as a baby, my dad fought with all the emotions one would expect a father to feel when he learns his child's body will not develop full function. There was grief, fear, and uncertainty. He told me he found me in my crib once with my limbs hyperextended in a position the doctors said to look for as a sign of the condition I have. On instinct, he quickly moved one of my arms out of the position as if that would change the reality he did not yet know how to face. After the diagnosis was confirmed, Dad came to my room again one night while I slept and prayed for me.

He heard the Holy Spirit say, *I have healed her spirit.*

It is curious that the Lord spoke this over me in the past tense at age one. Whatever that means, of this I am sure—the Holy Spirit raised me to know him. He healed my spirit. It has been responding to him ever since, pushing my soul in the direction of the Father's open arms. Even in times of disobedience, the Holy Spirit's conviction was near constant. It felt like he was saying to my soul, *I'm loving Jesus, Elizabeth. So keep up.*

PEOPLE ARE THREE-DIMENSIONAL

I am intentionally separating soul and spirit. Although there is debate on this topic in Christian theology, I hold the trichotomous view of humanity. There is biblical evidence that human beings are composed of three parts—spirits, souls, and bodies. Paul concludes his first letter to the Thessalonian church with this blessing:

> May God himself, the God of peace, sanctify you through and through. May your whole spirit, soul and body be kept blameless at the coming of our Lord Jesus Christ. The one who calls you is faithful, and he will do it. (1 Thess. 5:23–24)

The book of Hebrews shows a differentiation between soul and spirit:

> For the word of God is alive and active. Sharper than any double-edged sword, it penetrates even to dividing soul and spirit, joints and marrow; it judges the thoughts and attitudes of the heart. (Heb.4:12)

Paul also separates spirit from mind when he instructs the Corinthian church on the gift of tongues:

> For if I pray in a tongue, my spirit prays, but my mind is unfruitful. So what shall I do? I will pray with my spirit, but I will also pray with my understanding; I will sing with my spirit, but I will also sing with my understanding. (1 Cor. 14:14–15)

Paul is referring to praying or singing in words he and everyone else can understand and benefit from versus praying or singing with his spirit for which there is no understanding without interpretation.

What are spirits, souls, and bodies? Bodies are our physical frames—the cells, bones, and muscles we visibly see. Souls are our mind, will, and emotions. Spirits are the deepest parts of us that are regenerated and filled with the Holy Spirit when we surrender our lives to Jesus. Twentieth century Chinese church leader Watchman Nee relates these three parts of a person to the arrangement of the biblical temple. Nee writes,

> All these serve as images and shadows to a regenerated person. His spirit is like the holy of holies indwelt by God, where everything is carried on by faith, beyond the sight, sense, or understanding of the believing one. The soul resembles the holy place for it is amply enlightened with many rational thoughts and precepts, much knowledge and understanding

concerning the things in the ideational and material world. The body is comparable to the outer court, clearly visible to all. The body's actions may be seen by everyone.[77]

Nee's temple analogy connects us to the biblical story. We were individually and corporately made to be holy temples for God's Spirit to relationally dwell.[78] Remember the gospel of bidirectional access. The Spirit of God, who comes to live in our spirits at salvation, is the down payment of eternal life for believers in Jesus. Paul expresses this truth in his letter to the Ephesian church:

> And you also were included in Christ when you heard the message of truth, the gospel of your salvation. When you believed, you were marked in him with a seal, the promised Holy Spirit, who is a deposit guaranteeing our inheritance until the redemption of those who are God's possession—to the praise of his glory. (Eph. 1:13–14)

The inheritance alluded to is the time when the Father will unite all things in heaven and on earth in Jesus as the final outcome of the world's redemption accomplished through the cross. This includes anything not working well in our bodies and minds (or emotions).[79]

This Holy Spirit–life is our new life in Christ. The Holy Spirit empowers our lives for holiness because he re-establishes the image of God in humanity.[80] So Christians can affirm with Paul: "I have been crucified with Christ and I no longer live, but Christ lives in me. The life I now live in the body, I live by faith in the Son of God, who loved me and gave himself for me" (Gal. 2:20).

WHOLENESS FROM GOD'S PERSPECTIVE

Everyone has a spirit. If a person is born again through the saving power of the gospel, that spirit is alive. When we look at one another, we now have the opportunity to see according to God's perspective and to not base our attitudes upon other characteristics. Paul calls us to this accurate perspective of people, indicating, "So from now on we regard no one from a worldly point of view. Though we once regarded Christ in this way, we do so no longer" (2 Cor. 5:16).

The immediate context of this text is the correction of the human tendency to "take pride in what is seen rather than in what is in the heart" (2 Cor. 5:12). Paul is essentially screaming, "Corinthian church, get it together! It is the heart that matters!" Believers are all one in Christ because all our spirits are alive through the Holy Spirit. Only in seeing one another through the eyes of the Spirit of God can we unite together past our other differences.

If someone is not a Christian, we are not off the hook when it comes to seeing them from God's perspective. In obedience to the Scripture, we are to see *no one* based on a merely human understanding. Toward non-Christians, we can still see the potential God created when he designed them. God intends for people's spirits to be alive in Jesus. We have the joy of sharing with all people the glorious hope in Jesus to become fully alive. Sharing this gospel is how we participate with the Holy Spirit in "the ministry of reconciliation" as God restores humanity by removing the power and effects of sin, giving life to our spirits, and connecting us to his covenant family (2 Cor. 5:18). We are back to the Exodus God. Only this time, we share in an exodus from the slavery of sin through Jesus, the Passover Lamb, into a new covenant of relationship with God and each other.

DIGNITY FOR HIS DWELLING PLACE

In the early church, believers in Jesus contended against a false doctrine called Gnosticism. At its core, Gnosticism is the belief that some people have a special, higher knowledge gained through mystical secrets. These secrets supplant the Scripture and the gospel as the ultimate source of truth. Less than one hundred years after Jesus was resurrected, there were already groups of people emerging who claimed such secrets.

Gnostic teaching also elevated the spiritual aspect of a person over the physical body. Proponents taught that the body did not have any importance and denied that Jesus came in a physical body when he was on the earth. This false teaching produced errors in two directions: the brutal treatment of the body through ascetic rituals and the spiritualized permission to

The Dignity of Three-Dimensional Existence | 127

do whatever people wanted with their bodies. The confusion was so prevalent that the Holy Spirit motivated the apostle John to emphasize the difference between nascent Gnostic beliefs and Christianity. John writes to the church,

> Dear friends, do not believe every spirit, but test the spirits to see whether they are from God, because many false prophets have gone out into the world. This is how you can recognize the Spirit of God: *Every spirit that acknowledges that Jesus Christ has come in the flesh is from God.* (1 John 4:1–2, emphasis added)

Jesus's incarnation offers permanent dignity to the body. God himself redeemed all of humanity by living, dying, and resurrecting in one. Bodies, therefore, are not evil, ugly, or unimportant. They are designed for God's life in the same way that spirits are designed to be alive in Jesus.

It is no coincidence a primary test for the true Spirit of God is whether Jesus came in a physical body. God has made it clear that our bodies are just as important as our spirits and souls. While our spirits have the unique capacity to be filled with the presence of the Holy Spirit, we were designed to live this new-creation life in the Holy Spirit through our souls and bodies.

I do not want anyone to read the previous section and come away with the idea that I am promoting a Gnostic gospel. Seeing one another according to the Spirit is not a permission slip to do horrid acts to, or with, our bodies. Neither is it a denial of Jesus's incarnation. Biblical Christianity is the exact reverse of Gnostic beliefs. Spirits are not more important than bodies; spirits make bodies significant. Paul's question and answer in 1 Corinthians communicates this truth:

> Do you not know that your bodies are temples of the Holy Spirit, who is in you, whom you have received from God? You are not your own; you were bought at a price. *Therefore honor God with your bodies.* (1 Cor. 6:19–20, emphasis added)

For years, I did not like my body. I saw no reason to value something that only caused me pain and attempted to commit mutiny against my life plans. But my body is the Lord's tent, and if I despise his dwelling place, I dishonor him. God has been unalterably firm that I learn to love my body. He told me once, *I do not live in bad houses, and you are not a bad house for me.*

Another biblical test for the Spirit of God is whether someone confesses Jesus as Lord.[81] This confession is more than verbal acknowledgment. It includes the heart's dedication to live under Jesus's lordship. So I submit to Jesus in how I think about and treat my body. Despite my temptation to frustration, the Holy Spirit is delighted to live with me in this body. He likes his home and reminds me to take care of his temple. Every day, I choose again to love my body.

THE GOSPEL CANCELS STIGMA

The gospel is the ultimate solution to disability stigma. God sees much deeper than skin, muscles, bones, genetics, and neural pathways. People are hungry to be seen according to God's perspective rather than to standard human emphasis. This is true for everyone, disabled or not. But imagine how freeing this truth is to a group that is singularly defined by how "damaged" they are perceived to be.

The exodus from stigma is to live from the truth that a person's body and soul are only parts of them. The third part of a person, the spirit, is unaffected by the other two aspects of being. Through the power of God in the Messiah, our spirits become permanently whole. My spirit is the part of me in which the Holy Spirit dwells forever; my spirit is not disabled.

In charismatic circles, we teach there is no "junior Holy Spirit" regarding the ability of children to hear God's voice and minister in his gifts. There is no disabled Holy Spirit either. God is not limited in relationship with us by human limitations of any kind. In *The Perfect Gift: Seeing the Child, Not the Condition*, Chris Gore and Angela Locke record parents' firsthand testimonies of their children's healing of autism. While I celebrated the healings, I equally loved the testimonies of the experiences these little ones had with God. In one of the testimonies, Jesus taught a boy about communion through a dream.[82] In another, the Holy Spirit spoke the Father's love to a child who consistently repeated what he heard to his Mickey Mouse toy.[83]

Christian spirituality is not restricted by differences in cognition or socio-emotional processing. We must recognize the Holy Spirit in our brothers and sisters who have intellectual disabilities. Even though some may not be able to tell us their testimonies until eternity, God is more than able to communicate his gospel to their hearts and through their lives.

Healing does not jeopardize the talents God has placed inside us. This truth is beautifully illustrated in Brendan's testimony from *The Perfect Gift*. Brendan's mom describes a conversation she had with her son on the way to an event where Chris Gore would be speaking.

> On May 25, we were driving to the meeting and I said to Brendan, "Wouldn't it be cool if he prayed for you and your autism was gone?" He said to me, "Mom, one of the things I like about being autistic is that I'm creative. I don't want to stop being creative." He was afraid that if he were healed, that he would lose that part of his identity. I responded, "Creativity is a gift from God. Once he gives you a gift, he never takes it back! You can be healed from autism without losing your creativity!" He replied, "Awesome! I want that guy to pray for me!"[84]

This mother-son dialogue answers a question many people with disabilities have—to what extent is my disability me and how do I know the difference? It can be hard to separate the good gifts God has given us in our personality and skill sets from the conditions with which we are labeled.

I love what happens next in Brendan's story. When Chris prayed for Brendan, his mom describes,

> He didn't tarry a long in time prayer. He just quickly prayed and then what he did touched us so much. He asked Brendan to pray for him for more creativity. Here this man, who we consider to be a mighty man of God, is staying up late at night to pray for us, and he honored my son and us by recognizing what he saw on Brendan's life. It gave Brendan an opportunity to give back.[85]

It is so like Jesus to prophetically show Brendan's creative gifting to Chris so he can validate his little brother's heart as Jesus heals him. I am not surprised Chris holistically loved Brendan, responding to him apart from the disability. One of Chris's daughters has a disability, so he has years of practice, like my dad, seeing people according to the Spirit of God, not according to the flesh.

ARE WE TWO OR THREE PARTS?

Christians who value the gifts of the Holy Spirit are more likely to agree with the three-part person idea—we are body, soul, and spirit as described. It is difficult to explain the gift of tongues in an intelligible manner (pun fully intended) without the prerequisite concept of human beings having spirits. If we were not created with spirits differentiated from the mind or soul, how can Paul, and any of us along with him, pray and sing with our spirits as well as with our minds in 1 Corinthians 14:14–15?

I hold the trichotomy position, but I will give space to the other side. Dr. Wayne Grudem is a charismatic theologian, and he supports the two-part view. He argues, for example, that because *spirit* and *soul* are regularly used synonymously throughout Scripture, Paul could have easily substituted *soul* for *spirit* in his above explanation of the gift of tongues in 1 Corinthians. Grudem considers Paul to only be communicating that our soul, or inner life, can function outside of our conscious awareness.[86]

I could potentially agree with this concept because, at least partially, *soul* or *spirit* are defined outside of cognition. But as soon as we partially separate cognition from the soul or the spirit, we essentially end up with three parts anyway. No matter how we arrange the terminology, either three parts or a soul with separate functions, humans are more than a rational soul in a body. I could wax eloquently on the philosophical roots of the body-plus-rational-soul definition of *humanity* (thanks, Aristotle), but that would be breaking my earlier promise to not push us into the deep end of the philosophical pool.

Cognition First?
I find the two-part concept lends itself to a significant reduction in defining what it means to be human. In an interview with

Christian philosopher and scholar Dr. William Lane Craig on his new book *In Quest of the Historical Adam*, host Dr. Sean McDowell asks, "That raises the question, what does it mean to even be human? So, what's your understanding of what a human being is?"[87]

Dr. Craig responds,

> Well paradigmatically, we understand what it is to be human by ourselves. We look at ourselves. We know that we are human, and so we know what a paradigm of humanity looks like. Somebody like ourselves. So, there needs to be a certain anatomical similarity to us. That would mean that hominids in the past that didn't have adequate brain size, for example, would not be human. But mere anatomical similarity is not enough. What you want to look for would be those cognitive capacities that would be indicative of full human behavior. And here, there is quite a consensus among scientists about what those behaviors would be.... Like planning for the future, symbolic use of materials to represent nonphysical realities, advances in technology, inventiveness, and so forth.[88]

In fairness to Dr. Craig, he spoke anthropologically when he defined *humanity* here. The context of the statement was Craig's theory on the historical Adam based on integrating his biblical worldview with evolutionary biology. Craig was not thinking about disability and, hopefully, the above comment does not express his theological understanding of humanity. That said, the logic of his statement removes anyone with a significant intellectual disability from his concept of humanity. He makes cognition the ultimate marker of what makes us human. The moment we limit *human* to physical attributes, cognition, or behavior, we begin to close the worldview door on value for people with disabilities.

Now, I am not anti-intellectual. God gifted me with a great mind, and I desire to love him to the utmost with it. Three-part Christians can go too far and say the soul or mind is inferior to the spirit. That is not true. The Holy Spirit, living in our spirits, transforms our minds to think like Jesus. This is why Paul says, "We have the mind of Christ" (1 Cor. 2:16), and calls Christians to "renew your mind" with the truth of God's word instead of the world's ideas.[89] While there is no inferiority between soul and spirit, I do not derive my humanity from my mind or its capacity to reason. Humans are, after all, different from artificial intelligence robots who also possess a level of rationality.

Spirit First

In an article on the image of God and its implications for people with profound intellectual disability, professors Devan Stahl and John Kilner argue against defining the image of God based on specific attributes such as reason or the capacity to make moral choices. Rather, they argue that being made in the "image" and "likeness" of God (Gen. 1:26) indicates both a "special connection" to God and an "intended reflection" of his nature.[90] Stahl and Kilner write,

> People have a special connection with God and God intends them to reflect God's own attributes to the extent that they are able. The tremendous significance of human beings is completely secure, rooted in God's unwavering intentions rather than in variable current human capacities.[91]

The level at which people can reflect the qualities of his nature does not change God's intention toward them, his value for their lives, or his power to increase their capacity to reflect his attributes at any time.

I agree with the intended reflection concept and further define the *special connection* as the spirit that can relate to God independent of cognitive capacity. The three-part view of humanity holds the door open for this connection to God even when we may not be able to reflect God's attributes. It secures the value of the human race outside of any functional capacity and physical characteristics. Disability, physically or intellectually, never becomes a hindrance to respecting the image of God in any person. The two-part view could do the same if it adequately separates cognition within the soul. Instead, the two-part concept can over-spiritualize disability while minimizing earthly access to the triune God and intrinsic value outside of one's disability.

A THEOLOGY OF BROKENNESS

Some Christian theology identifies disabled people as gifts to the church to aid in its sanctification. In *Disability and the Gospel: How God Uses Our Brokenness to Display His Grace*, chaplain Michael Beates emphasizes this conclusion as he advocates for embracing a "theology of brokenness" toward the disability community.[92] Beates believes all people are valuable and the image of God in a person is unaffected by disability. On those conclusions, we agree.

In his theology of brokenness, Beates is applying reformed theology to create space for disabled people in the church, especially his daughter with physical and intellectual disabilities. Beates sees this theology as a way to close the "holiness gap"[93] between agreeing with Jesus's commands to include people with disabilities in the church and obeying those instructions. He notes healing will happen in heaven, but he argues that people with disabilities are a God-ordained blessing for the church's holiness against secular culture's idolization of strength, youth, and beauty.

I agree with Beates that secular culture has an idolization problem with strength and self-help. I disagree that God intends disability as the antidote to that idolatry. As someone who does not believe reformed salvation doctrines, (i.e., I am not a Calvinist), perhaps I've misunderstood Beates's argument. But as I read it, there are significant problems. He writes,

> Our spiritual worldview must be founded upon an understanding of our weakness wedded together with a much richer understanding of the sufficiency of grace. This is the starting place. And what more powerful illustration of weakness do we have than people who bear disabilities (either visibly in their bodies or undeniably in their manner)?[94]

Beates continues,

> In light of the secular discussion about and assault on personhood, as followers of Christ we must respect God's creation of all people and see them not as problems to be ignored or hidden away. Rather we must see them as mirrors of our own brokenness and as divine windows through which we can catch glimpses of God's grace. We must do whatever we can to respect God's image in even the most broken and twisted lives. Even the least of these carries intrinsic dignity and worth. When we see ourselves in their brokenness, we may apprehend the power of the gospel in our own broken and needy bodies and souls.[95]

This is an example of what can happen when theologies of disability drop the spirit of a person from the human equation. The spirit, and its potential for a relationship with God beyond cognition, never factored into Beates's analysis. So he had nothing to exhort Christian value for disabled people besides presenting disability as a somehow sanctifying reminder of human depravity. I could not disagree more strongly. My physical loss is not a mirror for anyone to look into and examine their sin. Jesus has made me whole, and someday, my body will experience that wholeness.

OBJECTIFYING WEAKNESS

I am all for recognizing my limits before God and my continual need for his all-sufficient grace, but it is not biblical love to objectify the weaknesses of other people—in this case, the disability community collectively—to reinforce that heart posture. Such a motive would be self-seeking at best and at worst contains an implicit utilitarian argument strange in a Christian worldview. Whenever we connect people's value to their usefulness to us, we error ethically. Moreover, the premise that the disability community is valuable because we inspire the nondisabled people to remember their weakness before God is degrading. It quickly becomes a form of negative inspiration porn where pity, not dignity, is the result. Again, perhaps I have misunderstood the conclusion and the logic behind it because it seems to fall far short of biblical love.

If I invited my non-Christian friends with disabilities to church using Beates's argument, it would be harmful and not in alignment with the truth of how God sees them and why God wants them in his family. I also cannot fathom approaching a fellow disabled Christian and saying, "Thank you for having a disability. It reminds me to stay humble before God." If the church needs the presence of people with disabilities to remain humbly submitted to Jesus, then we have bigger problems than justifying our outreach to them. We are called to humble ourselves before the Lord.[96] Disabled or not, no one can do that for us.

I find nothing in this concept that protects intrinsic worth, access to a relationship with God independent of cognition, or equality among believers based upon the Spirit of God in his people. Beates says "We must do whatever we can to respect God's image in even the most broken and twisted lives,"[97] implying this is a challenge we must grit our teeth to accomplish. If we see one another through the eyes and heart of the Father, there is no need for such a struggle. When all we see is brokenness via our theology, then indeed brokenness is all we will see.

The disability community does not exist to inspire anyone. Like all people, we were created for the Lord's pleasure and are valuable and desired by him solely on that basis. Jesus wants us in his church because we are people he died to save, not because we are object lessons for cosmic human weakness.

We are valuable because we carry the image of God, an image that is unmarred by the circumstances of disability. For those of us who cognitively can communicate our faith, we are fully alive in Jesus and fully whole, not broken. Our spirits are whole. For those with significant intellectual disabilities, like Beates's daughter, they are also spiritually whole in Jesus. The Holy Spirit can communicate the gospel to their hearts without cognition. Because their spirits are unaffected by their other limitations, they can connect equally to the Father, even if that connection cannot be fully expressed to the rest of us until eternity.

Beates's daughter should be included in the church because of who she is before the Father's face in Jesus—justified, holy, accepted, and a *subject* of his delight. She has a secure place in God's family forever and is not obligated to teach us something to be wanted and honored in God's house. This is a much better way to close Beates's holiness gap. There is enough grace to value all of God's beloved ones without resorting to arguments of utility revealing more of the world's pity than the gospel of the Messiah.

PITY VERSUS COMPASSION

The product of theology that celebrates the brokenness of people with disabilities is pity, and pity is birthed by pride. When I pity someone, I am separating my value from their value by the inflated recognition of how much more I have in comparison to them. I am above; they are below. This superiority mindset is why the disability community despises pity. We weary of a society that downgrades our personhood and value because of our limitations. We weary of pity that uses us for self-enhancement and self-congratulation.

Human compassion requires the establishment of equality first; it necessitates humility. Compassion between people is not a top-down offering. It is horizontal. When I show compassion to someone, I am serving them because I recognize their equal value and worth to my own. My actions and attitude will communicate this recognition. I am not helping them to congratulate myself on the good I have done, because I feel bad for the person's condition, or to earn some added benefit from their suffering. I am serving because I desire to protect and nurture their value. This horizontal, mutual dignity is inherent in the idea of "love your neighbor as yourself" (Mark 12:31).

Without the dignity of three-dimensional existence, compassion toward people with disabilities becomes dicey. Once we remove the concept that *in the image of God* includes the truth that everyone has a spirit that can relate with the Holy Spirit, we begin to slide into theologies of superiority toward disabled people.

The Spirit-filled church can uniquely give holistic theology to the disability community. I am a charismatic Christian because of access and this holistic theology. My physiological loss is not a limit upon my capacity to flourish in God's family. In this theology, I am respected, protected, and brought into the unity of believers. I am a whole person, even as my spirit has been made whole in Jesus.

THE WEIGHT OF GLORY

Returning to the temple metaphor, a born-again spirit becomes like the most holy place with the Spirit of God dwelling in our bodies. The fear of the Lord should be expressed in our recognition of this reality. There was discipline when the Israelites mismanaged the ark of the covenant and did not treat it with the proper care. Likewise, God still requires we are careful toward our brothers and sisters in Messiah, honoring and protecting what is sacred. Toward non-Christians also, we recognize they were made for the same redemptive purpose. Writer and theologian C. S. Lewis famously summarizes this truth in his essay, "The Weight of Glory":

> The load, or weight, or burden of my neighbour's glory should be laid daily on my back, a load so heavy that only humility can carry it, and the backs of the proud will be broken.[98]

The charismatic church is well-positioned to embrace this truth in practice. We believe God created us for his glory. We believe God loves to show us how he sees people. We have the honor of lifting others into their God-given identities and destinies as the Holy Spirit leads us to speak life and truth over them.

For people who claim we can see, we are often still hindered by our mindsets and preferences. We can always learn to see better as we encounter who God is in the Scripture and throughout our lives. The trouble begins when we stop asking to see because we think we already see fully. While there is great potential for the charismatic church to become a sanctuary where all people are seen according to the Spirit of God, the opposite is much more common, especially toward disabled people in our midst.

CHAPTER 8

Healing According to the Flesh

"Mom, these people don't want to be my friends ... They only want to pray for me to be healed!" I said between sobs into the phone. "I went to a gathering at somebody's house, and one of the guys prayed for me. But all he did was list the things that he thought were wrong with me! ... Why do they do that to me?" The sobs came heavy now, as the ice broke over an experience I had numbed.

"I'm so sorry," Mom said. "People don't know what they are doing."

My tears were in response to the following prayer: "God, heal the way she walks, moves, speaks, and thinks" plus other items on his long list I do not remember now. All I felt was humiliation. I shrank into the couch where I was sitting, barely able to utter a quiet "Thank you" and hoped he would not pray anymore. I thought, *Man, you have quite the list. Thank you for pointing all of that out to me, as if I was not already self-conscious enough.* I had a clear picture of how this man saw me, which was profoundly disconnected from how the triune God sees me. If my biological brother overheard that prayer, he would have quickly come to my defense. My heavenly brother was there instead, and without being any less protective, he recommended I forgive. It was done in ignorance, and I forgave.

After her reminder that people do not know what they do, Mom suggested, "Maybe you should not go to a charismatic church anymore."

After the call, I pondered her words. The suggestion came from the lips of someone who taught her daughter how to discern the voice of God, explained why the gift of tongues matters, and through example, demonstrated how to faithfully minister God's love and power to people's hearts. If she was suggesting it was time to turn the page, then there must be a real problem.

But asking me to leave charismatic Christianity was like suggesting I stop knowing how to breathe. The rising pressure of these thoughts came to a head as I turned my heart to the Holy Spirit and said in exasperation, "These are *your* people. Fix it!"

In reply, I heard a quiet question, *Why don't you explain it?*

This book is an attempt to obey that question. The first part of it, which you have finished, focuses on theology. The second part focuses on the practice of that theology. I am a charismatic Christian because of its theology despite how that theology is commonly practiced toward people with disabilities. Before I can call us into goodness, I must explain the negative practices and demonstrate why and how they harm. The young man who prayed for me thought he was doing good. He did not realize the pain he caused, and that is not his fault. I could not tell him because it was easier to numb the pain than try to make him understand it in a loud room crowded with people.

ONE-DIMENSIONAL

The T-shirts for the children's track at a conference were navy blue with three panels. Each panel was designed to look like the accessible parking symbol (i.e., the white line outline of a person in a wheelchair against a blue background). The first panel was a white stick figure in a wheelchair. The second panel was a stick figure praying for the stick figure in a wheelchair, and the third panel was a stick figure standing up in front of a wheelchair.

I am not one to be nitpicky about T-shirts, but this is a classic analogy for the reduction of being that occurs across the Spirit-filled church toward disability. Whoever made this shirt likely thought they made something cool. I anticipate their thinking to run like this: *Wheelchair. Jesus. Heal. Pray. Cool.*—without a clue about how the messaging in that design would be interpreted by people with disabilities.

First of all, the accessible parking symbol is about as reductive as it gets in disability descriptions. It is a one-dimensional outline of a half circle with the stick figure of a head, arm, and feet wedged on top of it. Despite its awkwardness, the symbol serves a critical purpose by not only designating parking but also accessible routes into buildings and a myriad of other accessibility features inside buildings. People with disabilities are always looking for these signs.

Culturally, that symbol also has value as a reminder of the accessibility achievements throughout the past half century. There was a time when those signs did not exist. I know that it is just a T-shirt, but if a disabled non-Christian saw that shirt, they would think that the accessibility sign was being mocked. The sign may not have any meaning to the able-bodied world beyond perhaps inconvenience, but it is meaningful to the disability community. The Spirit-filled church should not borrow it because it seems clever or funny to use.

More importantly, the messaging in the shirt instructs our children to see disabled people from one perspective only, their need for healing, rather than learning how to see people through God's heart. I value teaching our children to pray for physical healing. I always allow kids to pray for me because I want them to learn how to do it well, and they are often better than adults at praying with the Father's heart.

What we want to avoid is training them to think that God is only interested in healing people with disabilities. The "Wheelchair. Jesus. Heal. Pray." mindset is an incomplete and inadequate picture of the Father's heart. Our kids need to learn Jesus wants them to make friends with a disabled person just as much, if not more than, he wants to heal them. The opening story for this chapter could have turned out differently if the guy who prayed for me had chosen to spend time with me as a friend. If nothing else, he would have quickly learned there is nothing wrong with the way I think, even though my communication may be slightly different from his. That is why I cried to my mom that "these people do not want to be my friends." He did not see me as someone worth getting to know, only as an object to heal, and so he never tried to know me.

Last, I doubt the creators of the shirt considered there might be children with disabilities participating in the conference. They were thinking of healing as something the charismatic church does for "those people out there," not as something that would impact fellow brothers and sisters in Messiah. On the shirt, people with disabilities were depicted as *the other*, put in a separate category from everyone else. If, as a child, I was surrounded by throngs of other kids wearing that shirt, I would have felt embarrassment and shame.

GRACE FOR A HIGHER STANDARD

I have grace for people's ignorance. I have grace for people's lack of experience. I even have grace for people's prejudice. But in that grace, I am going to hold the Spirit-filled church to a much higher standard of behavior toward people with disabilities than the church at large and the world. We have the advantage of seeing with the Holy Spirit's eyes and of speaking it through prophecy. The guy whose prayer made me cry could have prophesied the Lord's heart for me first and then prayed for healing from that angle—if only he had thought about it.

In the previous chapter, we looked at the importance of seeing one another from three-dimensional wholeness, not from differences in external and internal abilities. Rather than seeing the disability community from wholeness first, though, the charismatic church has an extensive track record of downgrading people to their disabling conditions. Because of our value for supernatural healing, there is a tendency to switch the script, and just like in the world, disability takes on a false larger-than-life quality. Countless times, disabled people become what others behold in the flesh rather than anyone responding from, or agreeing with, God's perspective.

Through the years, I have said yes to prayer expecting to encounter heaven on earth, expecting to experience God's definition of reality and his perception of me. I've hoped for a beautiful gift, only to unwrap Becky Barbie again and again. Do not be surprised then that I've considered rejecting such gifts altogether. Some people have finalized that choice. The number one reason why people with disabilities are wary of charismatic Christians is because of how stigmatizing, and sometimes outright mean, we can be.

I have precious friends, Christians and non-Christians, whose bodies are visibly altered due to bone and muscle dysfunction. Although I acknowledge their disabilities, I do not see any of them as "broken" or "deformed." They are people God made and loves. I love them too. They are treasured ones for whom

Jesus intentionally shed his blood so they could have access to the Spirit of God who wants to live inside them. It grieves me that this perspective is not universal and that those I cherish are more than likely to be judged exclusively by their disabilities in the charismatic church as much as anywhere else on the earth. They remain one-dimensional—broken flesh. To exhort people to pray for healing, charismatic Christians practice healing tunnel vision.

HEALING TUNNEL VISION

We cannot afford to behave like the world and continue the systematic othering of those with disabilities merely because we believe in healing. We barely remember to ask people with disabilities if they are saved because of this tunnel vision. We have to keep first things first.

To illustrate the pervasiveness of healing tunnel vision, how many of us have stopped to consider whether somebody who visibly appears to need healing would like to receive the gift of tongues? If you are thinking, *I never thought about that*, then you see my point exactly. That would likely never be the first thing we think of because we zero in on healing to the loss of the other gifts of the Spirit, and what a loss that is.

While I have not received healing yet, I am beyond thankful to be able to pray in tongues. I pray in tongues the way I do because a friend asked the Lord to increase my prayer language. She did not see me one-dimensionally and wanted me to have all that is available in God's heart. A few days later in the middle of chapel worship at college, softly and near musically, out it came. I am so grateful.

The Holy Spirit and I enjoy joking together that I have perfected the art of *squeaking* in tongues. Yes, squeaking. I squeak at him whenever he overwhelms my heart's tenderness threshold. Unfortunately for me, the Holy Spirit has given me enough of the interpretation to know these heavenly squeaks run deeply counterproductive to deterring more of his sweetness.

Charismatic believers quickly assume that people with disabilities come to churches, conferences, or prayer meetings for healing. There is nothing wrong with coming to these spaces for healing, but it is wrong to presume that is the only reason why somebody is there. I come to prayer meetings to pray. I come to church to hear God's Word proclaimed, to be strengthened to live holy, and to connect with fellow Christians.

Statements like "I will not be satisfied unless Elizabeth leaves here walking" leave me with uncertainty and fear. My heart can profit nothing from them because I decided long ago to be satisfied in Jesus no matter what happens to me. These statements communicate that charismatic Christians are only interested in me as a potential demonstration of power, and I feel reduced to an object they demonstrate upon. It makes me question whether I am truly seen as a person, as a redeemed daughter, or as just the disabled girl present. Do people see me at all, or are they merely seeking manifestations of power to justify themselves?

People with disabilities do not exist for Christians to justify their ministries or their faith. We do not exist for people to be satisfied that, finally, we are seeing what has been promised in the Scripture. We do not exist for people's satisfaction. We exist for the Lord.

I never come to Christian gatherings exclusively because I want healing. I am there because I want to know God. I want to be among believers because that is where he is. When I am reduced to someone only there for healing, I feel denied the right to be there simply because God's presence is better than life. It is not that I have low expectations for God to heal me or that I am afraid to ask. I am glad to ask. But my heart does not turn on the fulcrum of my healing occurring like it is often assumed.

BOUNDARY VIOLATIONS

As we have already seen, many people with disabilities do not want healing prayers. They do not perceive themselves as needing change in any way and consider healing prayers as a judgment against their worth. Disagreement over these perspectives does not give us the right to bulldoze people's boundaries in the name of demonstrating God's power to heal. We do not represent Jesus in such behavior. It is common, however, for Spirit-filled Christians to criticize, or ignore altogether, the boundaries of disabled people who do not want prayer.

I have a friend, Jonathan, who is a Southern Baptist and a wheelchair user. I asked him once if he would allow me to pray for his healing when I am healed someday.

He said, "No, but if that happens, you can hug me with both of your arms."

I fully intend to hug my brother with both of my arms as soon as I can do so, and I would revisit this conversation at that point. But even if I stood before him, I would never force prayer on him. I would respect and love him without judging his heart. If healing is produced from that love, beautiful. If not, I would have still accurately represented Jesus.

Several years ago, I watched an online conference where a speaker told a crowd of thousands, "Go to the disabled parking places and wait for people. Do not even ask them if they want prayer. Just lay hands on them."

I promptly turned to my soon-to-be brother-in-law sitting beside me and said, "Don't ever do that."

Blake, who is one of the most respectful men on the planet, said he never would. I repeat, please do not do that. We must ask and wait for permission. Think of people like Emily Ladau and Amy Kenny. They do not want prayers for physical healing. If we violate people's boundaries, we are not expressing God's love.

It is fine to motivate people to pray for healing, but the above conference remark is not going to produce the miraculous. It creates a large potential for abuse by limiting disabled people to nothing more than healing projects or pending miracles. No one wants to be a project, and when we make people with disabilities our healing projects, we participate in stigma and lose sight of their value in God. Our ministry becomes about us and seeing the results we want, rather than wholehearted love for every person in front of us.

PLAY, DON'T PRAY

The children's hospital playroom had one rule: no one was allowed to discuss diagnoses, treatments, or anything related to why the children were in the hospital. This room was an intentionally dedicated space for kids to just be kids and, for a little while, to not have to think about the pain in their worlds. Hospital staff always explained the rule in advance to every volunteer group.

One church group signed up to play with the kids for an hour, but they came with a different agenda. Upon entering the playroom, the group paired off, made a beeline to each child, and began asking the parents specific questions about their children's diagnoses. This group gave all the children coloring-book pages titled "Jesus Healing the Paralyzed Man." They told the children Jesus was going to heal them and began touching and praying for them.

The kids were confused. The parents did not know how to respond. Some of the children were scared because they did not understand what *paralyzed* meant and thought it might happen to them. Hospital staff promptly removed the volunteers and told them they were not welcome in the playroom again.

One staff member who witnessed this is a dear friend. When she shared the story with me, Mama Bear Elizabeth was not happy. I was equal parts indignant, grieved, and embarrassed. Indignant because if Jesus had been in that playroom, the only thing he would have been doing was *playing*. Grieved because I can identify with the confusion of those little ones. In that space, they were probably not even aware of their difference. They were just playing, and their carefree moment was interrupted by the agenda of adults. Embarrassed because the volunteers were charismatic believers—my stream, my tribe—yet they presented a self-centered lack of perception in the name of Jesus and his healing power. It was wrong to assume any of these families had a Christian context. They may not have known who Jesus is, and they did not receive a fair introduction.

Some of you may be thinking, *I would never do that*. Good for you. Use your voices, influence, and platforms to make sure that actions like this do not happen. This is not behavior to be swept under the rug and ignored. It cannot be explained away with "They didn't mean anything by it" or "Their hearts were good." I cannot see into these people's hearts, but the actions appear selfish from the outside. It was all about them and what they wanted to do without a thought about how best to love these kids.

Others may be thinking, *If the children had been healed, it would not have been a problem*. Such a mindset is the problem and a rather heavy millstone. It presupposes that miraculous power should be elevated above loving and protecting children. It also assumes that Jesus would heal under those circumstances. God is not going to put his name and power behind such actions.

Children do not develop the cognitive capacity for social

comparison until approximately ages nine or ten.[99] While younger kids have some awareness of differences between themselves and others, they cannot fully assign substantive meaning to those differences. Their cognitive processes have not created the categories yet. We must be extremely careful, then, with our words in prayer over children. If they are younger than nine years old, they likely do not *know* they are different in the way adults see it. Kids just want to be loved. If they need healing, then we can love them into that experience. Most important, our posture toward them should reinforce that we will love them the same whether they are healed or not. Do not expect little ones to integrate that truth by default. They will not. It must be actively, intentionally communicated.

If Jesus planned to heal those children in the hospital that day, he would have done so while *enjoying* them—without asking a single question about what was "wrong" with their bodies and likely without even praying. If the volunteers had been walking by the Spirit, there may have been healing from the abundance of God's love and delight through them to the kids. It is high time to throw out the prayer formulas and become a people who overflow with the Holy Spirit in all we do. I wonder how many children Jesus has healed as he played with them.

VULNERABILITY

As a person's vulnerability increases, so does our responsibility to protect and respect boundaries. Along with children, we must protect the dignity of people with speech restrictions or intellectual disabilities. There is a tendency to ignore boundaries when praying for people with these types of conditions. Just because someone communicates differently or cannot communicate does not mean we have free rein to do whatever we want with them. No one will be healed at the cost of their value, and the Lord will hold all of us to the highest possible standard regarding how we treat the most vulnerable among us. We should walk in the holy fear of the Lord in this matter.

If someone has a speech restriction, the rules of human-to-human respect do not change. We are still required to ask for their permission to pray and touch them. This should be obvious, but it is not. These boundary violations happen in secular and Christian contexts, and they increase as the severity of disability increases. Such behavior is the fruit of impatience and ignorance that permeates the world, and it is not often corrected in the church. Communicative limitations do not make it appropriate to do whatever we feel in the moment, and boldness is not a valid excuse. Think about how it would feel if the roles were reversed. Imagine someone grabbing hold of you suddenly in a "moment of boldness" and shouting prayers over you without you being able to tell them to stop.

People with speech restrictions may use communication devices like pointing at laminated words or computerized equipment. They also rely on eye contact and nonverbal signals like nodding or shaking their head. Some of them can mouth words. Regardless of how they do it, most people can respond. It will just take a little extra time. Do not bypass checking in with them during prayer. Rather, we should check with them more often. If they are not comfortable with something that is happening, it will take them longer to interrupt and communicate. If you are unsure how a person communicates, ask. If we do not have the patience to ask and listen, then we are not walking in love.

Under stress, my disability does impact my speech, and healing prayer situations are usually high stress moments. Beyond the fear of people's poor responses, I fear their impatience if I challenge what is happening in prayer. It is common for people to interrupt or talk over me when I am having difficulty speaking. This only exacerbates the tension in my body and reinforces the problem.

Regarding those with intellectual disabilities, include them as much as possible. Most people have more ability than is at first perceived. Remember also that every person has a spirit. If a person cannot intellectually understand our prayers, their spirits are still engaged in what is happening.

CONFERENCE BOLDNESS

I volunteered to pass out name tags to ministry team volunteers at a daylong conference. Todd White was the keynote speaker. I had a great day meeting people, listening to their stories, talking about Jesus, and altogether enjoying myself. I chose to stay at the booth and not attend the teaching sessions though. In conferences, I become a healing dummy, a guinea pig for the miraculous.

Between the sessions, a group of young adults approached me. One of the guys asked, "Do you want to see something awesome?"

I knew he was parroting Todd. As my heart sunk in fearful dread, I said hesitantly, "Sure."

I did not experience God's love in their pursuit of my healing. No one cared to ask me my story, to learn anything about my heart, or to connect into Jesus's heart for me. They did not act in a way that would draw me closer to the God they believed in. I was only a pending miracle to them. At the end of ten long minutes, one of the girls was sobbing over me, telling me how much she wanted me to be healed. Then, I called the meeting to order, prayed for them, and sent them on their way.

I was likely the first person they saw in need of physical healing on the other side of the conference door, and they would have felt guilty to not pray for me. I can empathize with that feeling. When we are at a conference, our hearts are opened to new possibilities. In our zeal, we can lose sight of people in the name of our passion. I have been there many times myself, and I am relearning how to listen to the Holy Spirit as I minister his love to people. If I could redo this moment, I would have gently responded to the young man's initial question—"Do you want to see something awesome?"—with "You sound a lot like Todd White, but not Jesus. With whom would you most prefer to be identified?"

Todd gets a bad rap on the internet. I do not agree with all he says, but I respect him as a brother. I want to be clear that Todd is not the problem. I have listened to him over the years, and I have watched him grow in how he speaks about healing. I saw an interview where he teared up and had difficulty speaking in response to a story about healing ministry abuse (in this case, blaming disability on a person's sin or unbelief). After the story, Todd said, "Man, that story breaks my heart. That someone would be told that stuff. That's hard. I meet people every day with a history of that happening in their life. That's not okay."[100]

I believe Todd's heart is genuine toward people. I also hope Todd would rather people experience the heart of the Father than be healed at any cost, and it would probably break his heart that a group of young adults listening to him gave me no touchpoint into the Father's love. Todd would likely back up my statement that the goal is to sound like Jesus, not Todd, even if we feel emboldened from conference zeal.

Conferences are the least safe environment for me to receive healing. I would be more comfortable if someone prayed for me in public than in this setting. No, conferences do not count as public. In the West at least, they are in-house operations because most of the people there already follow Jesus. This actually makes them a more likely environment for abuse because all controls of acceptable behavior can come off without anybody knowing it. For example, someone walking past a person praying loudly for a wheelchair user at a conference will think, *Wow, look how bold they are.* When in reality, the person praying could be shredding the heart of the one on the receiving end.

In a public place like Walmart, there is protection because the praying would attract attention, and it would not automatically be assumed something good is happening. People would be watching, believers and nonbelievers. No one has ever prayed for me in public outside of church settings. I will immediately agree to prayer in that context because the purpose of the miraculous is to confirm the gospel to nonbelievers. There would also be a safe way for me to leave the situation if I needed to do so. But at conferences and other large gatherings, abuse is lost in crowds and loud music.

ABUSE

I learned early in life that to say no to healing prayer, or the way it is done, is to invite abuse. If I say no, there is pushback. This pushback is spiritualized as boldness, and then people with disabilities are judged for their resistance. It is okay to humbly ask a person why they do not want prayer and to engage in open conversation, but it is sin to pressure people who refuse prayer. I discussed this problem with a friend who said she always felt permission to say no when people asked to pray for her.

I responded, "You don't have a visible disability, so if you say no, people will not question your heart."

She replied, "Well, that's just abuse."

It is abuse, and abuse will never produce God's healing power. I once told somebody at a conference that I did not want to stand up and "test" her prayer. I was in an auditorium surrounded by thousands of people during worship. I had been worshiping God and was not aware of any circumstantial loss at that moment.

She interrupted my worship to pray, and I did not want to test anything. But I did because she responded to my refusal with "What do you have to lose?"

I think she was trying to get me to respond "in faith," whatever that meant to her, but all she did was bully me into compliance. In her mind, I probably did not have much to lose. In my mind, I lost all dignity. The subtext of her comment communicated to me: "If you don't try to stand up, you don't want your healing enough for it to happen." I could not endure the accusation, so I complied. She never saw little Elizabeth painstakingly crawl out of bed one night to try to stand "in faith" for healing. I had to call for Dad, who found me lying on the floor outside my bedroom door and helped me back to bed.

I am not fabricating the accusations either. I have been accused of not wanting my healing enough for it to happen. During prayer at a service, a man abruptly said, "You have to *want* it," emphasizing the word. My sixteen-year-old heart shattered. This man could never know the amount of time I have longed for healing—to climb a tree, drive a car, and make dinner for a husband. Nor could he understand the deep sorrow I experience because I cannot, and those are only a few things I do not know how to want more.

It took years for me to read John 5, the healing at the pool of Bethesda, without the pain of this memory washing over my heart afresh. In response, I have been motivated to search for the proper understanding of Jesus's question, "Do you want to be healed?" (John 5:6) and redeem it from the pit of interpretive misuse. Like the man healed in Lystra, there is more going on in this healing than we are apt to consider. The Exodus God shows up.

I've done so much research on this passage, I could not adequately do it justice here (see more on my website blog[101]). To summarize, Jesus's question seems directed at gauging and dislodging this man's hope in a superstitious healing power and redirecting it toward himself as the Messiah. I do not interpret it as a probe for faith, being categorically different from "Do you believe that I am able to do this?" (Matt. 9:28).

I will address the one time in Scripture, exclusive to Matthew's gospel, when Jesus asked two blind men the above question after they request healing. In reply, the men answer, "Yes, Lord," and Jesus touches their eyes to restore their sight (Matt. 9:27–31). The men's responses are significant. They believed Jesus was Lord, the Messiah, the son of David. They had been calling him *the son of David* before they followed him into a house and requested healing. He was Lord to them.

We are not Lord, and there is zero biblical evidence that suggests equal rights to ask this question. Jesus can ask it; we cannot. He gave us his authority to heal, not his authority to gauge faith for healing. When we presume this level of authority, we misuse Jesus's authority and abuse people.

The two traumatic experiences described above happened within a year of each other during my adolescence, and they had long-term effects. They planted a lie into my heart that I must accept prayer from everyone, even if I disagreed with what was being prayed over me. If I refused, I was scared to be accused again of not wanting healing enough. So it became easier to robotically comply. I allowed the young adults who parroted Todd White to pray for me only because I was afraid to say no and to face the backlashing pressure.

If someone asked the Father about the state of my heart in the past decade as groups of people surrounded me to pray, they would have found I was terrified most of the time. I was smart enough to spit out the response people wanted. But the real Elizabeth stopped responding. There was too much pain and fear. The numbness became automatic.

But no one seemed to care about my heart. Few people asked me or the Lord about it, and I lost the will to volunteer its tenderness to the slaughter of self-centered performance. The lie was allowed to germinate because it is all-too-easily confirmed when, as a movement, the Western Spirit-filled church follows Satan's temptation to set its affections on empty performance in healing ministry rather than on the love of God.

CHAPTER 9

A Love Affair with Performance

As Christians, we are supposed to be operationally defined by our love. Certainly, signs and wonders follow the sharing of the gospel.[102] But we are not to be distinctive by our power, but by our love. By our love, the world will know we are Jesus's disciples.[103]

Jesus warns that power without love easily results in deception. He says, "Many will say to me on that day, 'Lord, Lord, did we not prophesy in your name and in your name drive out demons and in your name perform many miracles?' Then I will tell them plainly, 'I never knew you. Away from me, you evildoers!'" (Matt. 7:22–23).

The "I never knew you" part relates to love. If we do not love, we do not live as people who know and are known by God.[104] If we divorce power from love, even if our ministry goals are successful, we get deception every time. This divorce is one of the reasons why the Western Spirit-filled church does not see as much of the miraculous as we would all like to see. Jesus is not going to give "greater works" (John 14:12) to a group of people who do not know how to love one another. He is not going to trust us with the power. The container has to be capable of containing the glory before he can fill it to its true capacity.

It can seem like every principle we know about respect, dignity, and love is thrown out the window when charismatic believers are in the mood to see dramatic healing. Suddenly, it becomes okay to violate people's boundaries for the goal of supernatural power. It does not matter what we say as long as we see the breakthrough. We start praying from earthly mindsets rather than from God's perception. None of these behaviors are loving, even if they are unintentional.

HOW SATAN HAS TWISTED THE STORY

Satan knows the power of miracle healing. He understands its power to confirm the gospel, and he has attempted to transform it into performance. He has twisted the story so we are tempted to pursue miracle power from mindsets of religious performance rather than faith in the Son of God, who heals freely.

The temptation to performance increases with visibility and severity of disability. Healings perceived to be dramatic, such as people with blindness seeing or people with paralysis walking, are sought after because they are mighty demonstrations of Jesus's power. Given the centrality of dramatic healings in the

Gospels and especially the mass salvations that follow them in Acts, Spirit-filled Christians are extra motivated to pursue them.

I want to take us back to the YouTube clip introduced in chapter 1 of the panel discussion among leaders in healing ministry. In the clip, Todd White shares about the problem of performance toward the disability community:

> Too many people have put the blame on somebody else of why they're not getting healed. Don't ever do that. Don't ever pray for somebody and say, "Listen, you just need more faith and then you will be healed." Jesus never did that. I've heard it from many people. I've noticed it more with people that are in wheelchairs, honestly, because I'll talk to somebody and pray for them, and I'll say to them, "Listen . . . I really want you to be made whole and I'm pressing so that this thing doesn't exist anymore." And they say, "Well, I'm really glad to hear you say that because a lot of people have told me that I need more faith and then I'll be walking." And it's in the church and it's big because we have to have a reason why not because we feel like we're in faith.[105]

I'm thankful Todd publicly pointed out this dynamic. I add that the temptation to blame a disabled person for lack of healing extends beyond those with mobility disabilities to include anyone who needs visible healing or a dramatic miracle.

THE PROBLEM LIES WITH ME?

There have been decades of corrective teaching in the charismatic church against the spiritual abuse of this blame game. Increasingly fewer charismatic believers would tell somebody they are not healed because of their lack of faith. That exact language is not used anymore for the most part.

Heart posture takes longer to reset than word choice, though, and the mindset that it is the fault of the disability community for not receiving healing has continued in more subtle forms. The problem-lies-with-me narrative remains strong. I heard a sermon once that reinforced this narrative. The pastor used the story of Jesus healing Bartimaeus, emphasizing how Bartimaeus threw off his beggar cloak after Jesus called him to come. The pastor explained that Bartimaeus removed his beggar identity because he knew Jesus would heal him from blindness. Then he says, "Some people don't get healed because they are attached to the identity of their sickness." I heard the audience's agreement as my heart plummeted. I knew people would take that phrase and run with it, calling the idea *wisdom* as they use it against those who are not healed.

The application is problematic. Yes, Bartimaeus threw off his cloak in Mark's gospel when people in the crowd say, "Cheer up! On your feet! He's calling you" (Mark 10:49). Would we not all be excited to hear someone say Jesus is calling for us? Would our hope not soar? It is strange to use a story of one man's excited delight over Jesus's response to his call as a generalizable knife against people who are not healed.

While many disabled people consider disability to be an identity, if someone has come forward for prayer or has allowed prayer, it is logical to assume disability identity is not a factor in the equation. Even if it is, the Holy Spirit can correct that factor if it is really in the way of how he wants to love the person.

Here in Mark 10, Jesus does not seem moved in any measure by the fact that Bartimaeus removed his cloak. When he approaches, in verse 51, Jesus asks him, "What do you want me to do for you?" He did not assume anything about this man, even though it is obvious Bartimaeus is blind. Jesus can see just fine, but he still seeks out Bartimaeus's heart's request. He says, "Rabbi, I want to see," and Jesus heals him.

Jesus responds to a request motivated by the recognition of his identity as the Messiah. Bartimaeus got Jesus's attention in the first place because in verse 47 he was shouting after him, "Jesus, Son of David, have mercy on me!" In contrast to the crowd who could see Jesus with their physical eyes, Bartimaeus recognized the Messiah without seeing him and placed all his trust in Jesus's identity as such. He calls after the Lord first and takes off his cloak only because Jesus calls back.

The significance and glory of this healing are centered on Jesus's identity as the son of David, not Bartimaeus's identity via the removal of his cloak. Matthew and Luke never mention the cloak when they share this healing because Bartimaeus's cloak is not central to the ultimate message of the passage. When we turn healing ministry into performance, we emphasize the unimportant to the loss of what truly matters, namely the glorification of Jesus as the Messiah.

SATAN'S PLAYLIST OF CONDEMNATION

Blaming people for not receiving healing can sound like, "You don't have enough faith." But it also sounds like the following:

- "You have to want it."
- "Your disability has become your identity."
- "You're not laying hold of it."
- "You can't receive healing."
- "You must be benefiting from your disability."
- "You're in agreement with your disability."

Along with stigma, the persistence of the problem-lies-with-me narrative is another reason why there are so few Christians with disabilities in charismatic spaces. Nobody wants to face those accusations, and few can carry such a heavy burden for long, especially if there is no one willing to lift it off.

During a prayer experience for my healing, one of the three people praying began to pace around the room with a stern expression on his face. As he paced, he said sharply over and over, "Talk to her, Lord. Talk to her. Talk to her, Lord." He never explained what he was asking the Lord to talk to me about, and

I was too afraid to ask. He left visibly frustrated, while I was bewildered.

My mind filled in the blank of the question I was scared to ask. I interpreted this person asking the Lord to talk to me about having more faith for healing. I perceived this man to be communicating that the reason I was not healed was because there must be something wrong with me, my understanding, or my communication with the Father. Maybe this was not the case, but because of the man's harsh demeanor, I was not brave enough to ask him to explain. I received no love in the above interaction, only confirmation of my worst fears.

The problem-lies-with-me narrative, with all its diverse phrasing, is Satan's playlist of condemnation. The narrative comes straight from his heart, not the Father's heart. When we use it in healing ministry, we give Satan ammunition against people, and he will use whatever we give him.

If I am not healed, those praying can remove themselves from the circumstances. They will go to bed and forget that my body exists, but I will go to bed aware of it. And once again, it has become "an opportune time"[106] for Satan to accuse me and God. This is expected. I now have maturity and wisdom in the Lord to resolve the difficulty. I took the pain of the above experience directly to the Father that night, and he talked to me about it.

But I do face the accusations. As a child and a teenager, I did not have the same level of understanding. We best be protective of our youth and new believers when we pray for healing. We have to be able to contextualize "not being healed" for them—not to excuse the absence of power, but to protect them from Satan's accusations. We cannot leave the lambs defenseless before the wolves. At the very least, we must teach them how to take disappointment to the Lord. Those praying for me have often been too busy nursing their own disappointments and insecurities to show me how to yield mine to Jesus. If it was not for godly parents, I would have only internalized the lies with no opportunity for their dismantling. Not everyone has that luxury.

As a child, I remember asking one Sunday at church, "Daddy, did I do something wrong so that I can't walk?"

"No, Lizzie. You didn't do anything wrong," Dad said. Then, he explained that disability happens because we live in a broken world while living in the kingdom of God, a kingdom that is both here and not yet present in all its fullness.

I do not know what thoughts led to this question, only that I asked it. I needed someone to tell me that whatever the *why* behind the suffering, it was not my fault for causing or continuing it. Sometimes when the pain is bad, I still ask the heavenly Father the same question: "Abba, I do not understand what is happening here. Did I do something wrong?" He reassures me I have not and comforts his Little Seed again.

I am not the only person who asks, "Why am I hurting?" All people ask this question. The performance narrative, no matter how spiritual we make it sound, gives the wrong answer. As those full of the Holy Spirit, we should give a biblical answer rather than blaming people for their pain.

LOUD RIGIDITY

Performance mindsets lead us away from love and toward following rigid prayer formulas that produce no life for the person who prays or for those receiving prayer. It is easier to zero in on one "right way" to pray for healing than it is to have biblical trust in God's power to heal. While it is good to use examples of supernatural healing found in the Bible as ways to pray for healing, we should not replace demonstrating the heart of God with a zealous pursuit of one type of prayer. Healing power is released through love, not by following formulas.

As someone with a type of paralysis, a common prayer for my healing is people commanding me to "get up and walk!" The issue of volume in prayer is personal because my body produces a severe startle reflex. When others shout commands at or over me, my body spasms. People then think it is either a manifestation of the Holy Spirit or perhaps a demon, and as quickly as my reflexes allow, I correct the assumption. The response would be the same if somebody yelled "cheeses!" or "Jesus!" suddenly in my presence. It is not the Lord, and it is not a demon. It is simply a reflex that never integrated neurologically after infancy. We swaddle our babies to help them sleep because of this same reflex.

The statement "get up and walk" is biblical. In all four Gospels, there is an account of Jesus healing a man by speaking a similar phrase.[107] The healing accounts in Matthew, Mark, and Luke are the same while the one in John is a separate incident.

There is profound revelation of Jesus's beauty and goodness in these healings. In Acts, there are two records of similar healings: the man healed at the temple and the man at Lystra. Whenever the Bible repeats something, it is God's way of highlighting its importance. The Holy Spirit is flagging something for our attention.

So what does God want us to know and understand about who he is from these healings? I see three truths automatically:

1. God is revealed as the healer.
2. God heals people no one else can restore (e.g., permanent paralysis).[108]
3. One of the ways God heals is through his voice.

After all, Jesus is "the Word" (John 1:1). He spoke the universe into existence. It makes sense God would move in power through spoken words.

COMMAND OR INVITATION?

The issue develops when we perform with our words. We often think the louder, more forcefully we say something, the more faith or authority we demonstrate. Volume and faith are not equivalent. If they were, then Jesus had a faith problem. Matthew connects Jesus's healing ministry to a beautiful prophecy from Isaiah:

Jesus, aware of this, withdrew from there. And many followed him, and *he healed them all* and ordered them not to make him known. This was to fulfill what was spoken by the prophet Isaiah:

> "Behold, my servant whom I have chosen,
>   my beloved with whom my soul is well pleased.
> I will put my Spirit upon him,
>   and he will proclaim justice to the Gentiles.
> He will not quarrel or cry aloud,
>   nor will anyone hear his voice in the streets;
> a bruised reed he will not break,
>   and a smoldering wick he will not quench,
> until he brings justice to victory;
>   and in his name the Gentiles will hope."
> (Matt. 12:15–21 ESV, emphasis added)

In the context of his healing ministry, Matthew emphasizes the Messiah's humility. Rather than using miracles to magnify himself, Jesus healed from a posture of gentleness. Too often, we get loud because we are insecure in our identity and we are desperate for a power display to prove ourselves before ourselves and others.

Unlike us, Jesus does not allow the attention of miracle power to influence his identity before the Father or to interrupt the Father's mission, which will ultimately culminate in death and resurrection. Jesus brings his proclamation of justice to the nations through this humble surrender to the Father and an attitude of tenderness toward weakness in the human condition. This is his path to bring justice to victory.

Biblically, there is a time and place to raise our voices. We see two ministry scenarios in which Jesus does so. He rebukes demons sharply,[109] and he raises Lazarus from the dead with a loud voice.[110] Outside of the demonic and Lazarus, there is no indication Jesus yelled or raised his voice toward anyone while displaying supernatural power. I have great news. The disability community is neither demonized nor dead, so we can stop shouting.

Even in the drama of raising the dead, volume is not always required. When Jesus raises Jairus's daughter, he reveals the gentleness of the Father. Jesus simply takes her hand and says, "Little girl, I say to you, get up."[111] It is hard to imagine a softer sentence. I often wonder if there is faith left in the charismatic movement for tender demonstrations of power.

The statement "get up and walk" may be more accurately interpreted as an invitation than an aggressive command. Jesus is speaking imperatively, but we do not find changes in tone or volume noted in the Scripture. Rather than assuming a loud tone, we should at least consider he spoke in a normal voice.

At the temple, Peter and John imitate this same invitational stance from their rabbi. Peter was straightforward about the situation. He did not have any money for the man at the gate, but he freely gave what he did have—healing by faith in the name of Jesus. As a result of the testimony from that miracle, the newly birthed church nearly doubled in size.[112] This was all because of a gift, the provision of supernatural wealth to cancel the poverty in a man's hurting body.

The next time we pray for someone with paralysis, we have permission to be like these first disciples and imitate Jesus. Look the person in the eyes, smile, and invite them to stand. If someone treated me with gentleness in this way, I would put my hands in theirs and try to stand. I can put my faith and hope in the kind invitation of God.

I use the example of paralysis only because "get up and walk" is what I know, but the same scenario can happen with any other condition. Jesus did not yell at those with blindness to see, nor did he shout at deaf ears to open. He invited the man with the shriveled hand to simply stretch it out. There was no fanfare or hype. No performance. Jesus gave healing as a gift.

Pop quiz! I have already mentioned a moment in Acts when a follower of Jesus spoke with a loud voice to heal someone. True or false? (Hint: the healing happened during a public sermon, and it caused quite a ruckus.)

True. Paul healed loudly in Lystra.[113] In submission to the Scripture, it is okay to raise our voices under the Holy Spirit's leading and in appropriate settings. The one time there was a loud healing in the Scripture was during a public message. Paul interrupted his sermon to heal a man who could not walk. Paul was not likely close to the man's face, and in this divinely orchestrated moment, it was fine for Paul to use an outdoor voice. Like Paul, we can follow the Holy Spirit and be mindful of the setting around us while remembering God is not more likely to answer our prayers based on the volume and tone of our voices.

TEST PRAYER CONSIDERATELY

If we invite somebody to stand and walk, it is logical we would help them to stand. When done respectfully, this is biblical and good. When we are operating from religious performance though, it can be harmful and keep us bound to the blame narrative if there is no breakthrough. We cannot use testing prayer as proof of someone's character or faith. We have no authority to do that. If people do not want to try to stand or attempt another suggested action, it is abusive to pressure them to do so and prideful to criticize their hearts if they refuse.

Each person's circumstances are different, and individual needs must be treated with care. Some people's bones break easily. Others have sensory processing differences and prefer to not be touched. Some may not understand what is happening, or it may be more difficult for them to speak. As we partner with God for healing, we must be considerate and honoring. The Holy Spirit is the most considerate, respectful person I've ever met. Yes, he is also "a consuming fire,"[114] and his jealous heart is fierce. Whichever facet of his glorious character is under emphasis, he knows what he is doing. We should obey him.

Speaking of obedience, do not use the example of Naaman's healing from leprosy[115] when discussing willingness to test the effectiveness of prayer. When we apply this story to pressure anyone into performing an action, we step into manipulation and control. Each one of us is responsible for obeying the Lord, but this is not the same as agreeing with whatever someone tells us to do. We sin when we "play God" toward the heart of another person, and referencing a biblical text to justify ourselves does not make this attitude any less sinful. Again, Jesus gave us his authority to heal, not the authority to pressure people to do what we say. God's healing power never comes from control.

Some settings are not appropriate for the intensive testing of prayer. During a live prayer-and-worship set, I allowed a young man to pray for my healing. I was alone and sitting in the front near the stage. I had been enjoying time with the Lord, and my first thought when he asked to pray was, *Honey, I'm a little busy right now.* His eyes were so earnest, though, so I let him pray. After a few minutes, he asked if I would try to stand. This was one of the few times I bravely said no.

I looked him straight in the eyes and said, "You would have to hold me up, and I am not comfortable with that." I added internally, *And there is* no way *I am getting in your arms.*

I watched the wheels turn in his head for a moment, and then he said, "I understand." He prayed a few minutes longer and then went on his way.

Although I do not doubt that this man's heart was pure, I am thankful he did not push against my boundaries. If strangers are praying for me, I will only allow a woman to help me stand. In this instance, though, I would not have wanted to try standing if a woman was available. I did not want to distract the people leading worship a few feet from me or those praying around me in the room. Setting matters. This was not the right space to test for healing by standing, and that is okay.

A better way to check for healing is to ask if the person can try to do any action they could not do previously. Keeping options open allows people to choose what they are most comfortable doing. For example, it is much easier for me to try to move my shoulders than to stand. I know what the standard range of motion is in my shoulders and can report any change. People with physical disabilities are usually keenly aware of their bodies. It is not hard for us to find a way to check that is safe. Respectful, flexible partnership protects against performance.

PARTNERSHIP NOT PRESUMPTION

The kindest question someone asked me before praying for healing was "Has the Lord told you anything about your healing?" I answered it honestly, sharing a conversation the Lord and I had on the subject. This type of question opens the door for partnership between my heart, the Lord's heart, and the brother or sister praying. Everyone involved can come into agreement together now. It is also protective because I no longer have to screen for, or run interference against, abuse. The question offers me agency and a place in God's heart to rest my faith. This brother and I prayed together. I was not healed, but I retained my value. I left encouraged, thankful there is another person in the world who believes *with me*.

A valid question should be raised at this point. What about all the people we pray for who do not have a relationship with God? We would not normally go around asking questions like that on the street. Correct. This scenario will not work in every context. I would not ask somebody on the street this question unless the Holy Spirit directly prompted me to ask. The Holy Spirit understands the context of everything.

The next question I anticipate is "What if I don't hear anything?" Wait on him a moment. We get in a hurry sometimes. I caution against praying for healing without the capacity to listen and obey. If hearing God's voice is a problem, maybe address that with him before becoming heavily involved in supernatural ministry. Hearing and obeying the Father is not optional. It is imperative for all of us.

There are times, though, when we may not hear anything specific. If so, go to love and we will at least be headed straight. It is okay to take someone's hand and simply pray, "Father, thank you for loving this person. I release your healing power and heart of love for them in Jesus's name."

COMPASSIONATE CREATIVITY

For years, I thought as long as I did everything others told me to do in prayer, I had the best chance of being healed and, most important, of protecting myself from accusation. I thought it was my duty to say yes to every offer of prayer, agree with everything said, and participate in every test. Experience taught me that to say no in these circumstances would invite judgment, and I believed the judgment. I believed it would be my fault if I did not do it all just right.

I also thought the experience of healing was one-dimensional. I'd heard stories of people receiving healing who said they felt electricity going through their bodies, the power of God surging through them. As someone who lives in chronic nerve pain with "electricity" shooting through my body daily, I used to be afraid during prayer of the healing experience itself. Intellectually, I would have said I did not expect the Lord to hurt me, but my heart could not differentiate what God's power might feel like from the long-term trauma in my nervous system.

In September 2019, I told the Lord the electricity description of healing sounded like nerve pain to me. I asked if that was the only way he could do it, adding that if so, I was willing to submit. In a tone of deep tenderness, I heard him say, *I'm not gonna hurt you.*

"Okay, but does it have to feel like that?" I asked further. "The only context I have is pain."

What do you want it to feel like? he asked.

I paused to consider the magnitude of his question as the embers of hope, trust, and childlike affection kindled afresh within me. The warmth of his goodness began to thaw my heart's numbness.

"How about warm oil?" I asked, thinking how soothing that would feel to my nerves and muscles.

The Lord chuckled softly in my heart, and then said, *Well, it's biblical.*

A few minutes later, with my heart imploding from the implications of this exchange, I said, "Lord, I am so honored you would ask me that. I did not know you cared about that."

Of course, he whispered. *I love you.*

Like the arrow in the FedEx logo, I see oil everywhere in the Scripture now, and I am not afraid of the Lord's touch anymore. It is no surprise that I requested warm oil. Two years before, the Holy Spirit wooed me with a similar proposition. I'd been living in the basement of the Father's heart, and the Holy Spirit wanted me to relocate.

He said, *You'll like it upstairs* (i.e., a metaphor for closer to his heart). *There is lots of warm oil.* He probably chuckled at the resonance between these parallel exchanges.

The Holy Spirit did not guarantee exactly what healing would be like, and I am not in charge. He simply asked for my input. Notice, though, the Lord did not rebuke me for being afraid or scoff at me for asking if there were options. He did not trap me in a corner where I had to accept one way to be healed or lose the chance. We all have tender places in our hearts that respond based on our experiences, even if the responses cut against the grain of what we know is intellectually correct. God cares about these tender places.

This conversation taught me healing is not a one-size-fits-all system to be rigidly administered. God enjoys being creative toward us. He knows each one of our hearts and is attentive to the best way to heal any type of pain. Like a cup with his oil poured over our lives, God's heart brims over with compassionate creativity to heal us.

There is spiritual warfare against this childlike faith for flexibility in healing. The devil does not want any of us to partner with God's creative affection. When pondering the above dialogue, I sometimes hear this scoffing, derisive thought: *You just want it to be sweet.*

Yes. Sweetness is allowed. God's love expressed in his healing power can be sweet—for me and many others. I am hoping when Jesus heals us, we will encounter the Messiah who brings justice to victory by dealing gently with those he restores. Healing does not have to be as bitter as Satan wants us to think by trapping us into performance-based religious systems.

In the next chapter, we turn our attention to a model of healing ministry overly focused on the bitterness of the enemy's work to the loss of the kind, compassionate, and altogether lovely work of God.

CHAPTER 10

Trading Heaven's Glory to Magnify Hell

There is a type of healing ministry that is overly devil-focused. It attributes sickness or disability and its continuation to be connected with spiritual forces of darkness that people have permitted in their lives. Not only are people with disabilities physically broken, but we are also oppressed by spiritual darkness, whether we are conscious of it.

I am not opposed to deliverance ministry. Deliverance has its place in a supernatural lifestyle. I am opposed to foolishly, and unnecessarily, conflating healing and deliverance together. I'm pulling the theological emergency break over this problem because someone has to reset the paradigm before we mangle hearts in the looming crash. I have read one too many stories of the anguish produced in the hearts of disabled people when they are assumed to be under demonic influence. I am no stranger to that bitterness.

Someone once asked me to break a spirit of infirmity from my family bloodline. I challenged why I had to break an agreement with my bloodline if Jesus already accomplished full redemption for my healing. In response, there was pushback, not humility. I was told that even though I had nothing to do with it personally, I needed to break the agreement because there was a generational spirit of infirmity in my family. The implication was that this spirit was preventing my healing and that it was up to me to change my circumstances.

Because I understand the basic assumptions in this theology, I can at least attempt to give people the benefit of the doubt that they do not mean to curse me or blame my family for the suffering in my body. I can do the worldview gymnastics required to be merciful to people who pray like this, but when these types of prayers occur, they tear my heart open. No one should be in a position of trying to decipher whether someone is cursing us during prayer. There will be exponential harm if this type of prayer is practiced toward a person who has a body like mine and zero context, such as a secular disabled person.

Situations like the one above move beyond stigma to blaming disability on families and individuals for its continuance. These prayer emphases are only from a negative perspective and provide no access to God's perception of the person. Just because I have a visible condition while someone else has normal body function, that does not mean there is more spiritual darkness in my family line than theirs. The effects of the fall are universal. If we look back far enough into everyone's family, we would see brokenness and dysfunction. Why are we looking back like that when we could be looking at Jesus? I have no idea.

A RELIGIOUS SYSTEM

Through the next minutes of this prayer or exorcism, I complied because I was terrified to refuse. If I refused, I was scared I would be accused of being further complicit with that generational spirit and of preventing my healing. I was afraid these people would leave my house, thinking, *No wonder she's not healed. She can't let go of the curse.* I also knew Satan would back up that line of thinking later when the time came to attack my heart. There had already been pushback when I attempted to disagree, so I violated my conscience to please people and avoid abuse.

That day through today, I am only interested in one bloodline—the one I've been graciously grafted into in Jesus.[116] My bloodline is the purest it could ever be. Yes, sin produced brokenness in the created world, but then Jesus died and resurrected. I do not need to break agreement again with what my savior has already crushed.

The counterargument is I am supposed to use my faith to reject the curse Jesus has already broken so that I may be healed. But now the emphasis is on my performance instead of on Jesus's love and power. And again, my bloodline is pure now and forever, irrespective of what my body looks like. I will not put my faith behind what is false.

Imagine Jesus kneeling in front of me, reaching out to touch me. But suddenly he stops and says, *Oh sorry, Sweetheart, I can't heal you. There is just too much disease or darkness in your family history. You'll have to clean that up first.*

Never. Not Jesus. This style of healing ministry is a religious system that is not gospel-centered. Healing is about God's power, not the power of Satan. I understand some situations are a bit more nuanced. I am not referring here to legitimate demonic deliverance. Demons are real, but people with disabilities need healing for physiological loss, not demonic activity. If there is a demon, we should get rid of it. However, there is a real, tangible difference between healing and deliverance ministry. We participate in great carelessness with both prophetic and healing gifts when we try to find the supposed demonic stronghold behind every disability.

A TRIPLE BIND

Time and again, people have told me to renounce my diagnosis or to break agreement with it, assuming this action will communicate to the influencing demonic forces that I am opposed to them and finally using my authority in the Messiah so the disability will stop. Usually, they start asking me to do these types of things when their original prayers have not worked. The pattern is consistent. The prayers are not working, so there must be something demonic in the way. People also rebuke my diagnosis or tell it to leave my body, thinking there is an evil force attached to it.

Nothing could be further from the truth. The condition in my body is not demonically influenced. The medical diagnosis does not have any spiritual substance or significance. It is a description of a biomechanical deficit I need Jesus to restore. I need Jesus to rewire me, to re-create my nerve cells. I do not need to break collusion with demons for Jesus to accomplish that re-creation. I have made no agreement with darkness to produce or continue my circumstances. I was just born. I am innocent.

The next counterargument is if I wanted my healing enough, I would be willing to try anything. That is a dangerous mindset. I am not willing to try *anything*. I am only willing to follow the Messiah, and I was taught to run away from the voices of strangers.

The only fruit that connecting disability to the demonic will produce is to drive the hearts of disabled people who do not know Jesus farther away from him. We are Jesus's representatives to a lost and dying world. If this is how we treat them, they will believe Jesus associates them with evil. I speak the truth. That is what disabled people think about charismatic believers who emphasize the demonic toward them. What else are they to think?

When I am asked to renounce, break agreement with my disability, or break off spirits, I obey because I am stuck in a brutal triple bind. If I refuse, people will only be further confirmed in the mindset that I am complicit with darkness and have made my disability into a supernatural stronghold I cannot release. As a second shackle, Satan will accuse me later of preventing it if

I do not comply. The third chain is when people challenge my hesitation or push back against my concerns, there is enough self-doubt in me to consider that maybe I will be resisting God if I do not go along with it. Jesus would never tie me in a bond like that.

My mom once encouraged me to tell people I've already broken all these types of agreements before they start praying.

I replied, "No, that only gives power to that perspective."

Mom responded, "But that is the only way to get them to stop."

She's right. In the absence of humility, the only way to avoid abuse is to falsely agree.

While teaching for a United Kingdom evangelism conference, Eric Gilmour emphasized displaying the beauty of Jesus when we share the gospel. Toward the end of the teaching, he says, "The last thing we want to do is trap them in a corner and collect their consent."[117] As soon as the words left his lips, I thought of this chapter. That is exactly what is happening with these devil-focused emphases.

THE BEST OF BLOODLINES

Especially toward people with genetic disabilities, bloodline and infirmity prayers are attractive because they appear to be logical. The question is, logical for whom and to what purpose? My disability is not genetic, but I see the faces of beloved friends whose conditions are genetic and who currently live outside of relationship with Jesus. My blood runs hot when I think about charismatic Christians pressuring them in the Lord's name to renounce curses or spiritual darkness in their bloodlines to receive healing.

If the goal is biblical healing power, I do not see the logic in this approach. Nowhere in the Gospels or in Acts do we see miracle healing come from attempts to cleanse bloodlines or renounce spirits of darkness. I understand this is a claim from silence, so I am not arguing against such approaches in all cases. Rather, we must stop applying these ideas carte blanche. The Bible does not teach that there are demonic links to most disabling conditions.

The moment we yield to the Lord for salvation, we become a new creation. Paul is absolutely clear on this: "Therefore, if anyone is in Christ, he is a new creation; old things have passed away; behold, all things have become new" (2 Cor. 5:17 NKJV). How many things? All things! Most of the time, the Spirit-filled church does a great job at calling us to live submitted to the righteous identity Jesus provides. There is no need to regress to the slavery of sin-bound existence in healing ministry.

In the Messiah, we die to whatever is present in the first Adam's bloodline—sin, darkness, and spiritual death. We rise again with a new DNA, the life of the second Adam—that is, the Messiah himself in us through the Holy Spirit.[118] We enter the best of bloodlines. Biblically then, the way to clean a bloodline is to be born again. We should put first things first.

There are thousands of natural causes of disability. It is grossly inaccurate, biblically and practically, to attribute the cause to the demonic automatically. The harm can be lasting, so be aware there is little room to be incorrect if we pray in such a manner. If we are not absolutely sure the Lord is taking a healing situation toward deliverance (i.e., a real demonic manifestation), we need to think twice.

SPIRIT OF INFIRMITY

Spirit of infirmity is a go-to prayer, more common than "get up and walk." People pray it ad nauseam over me because they think it is spiritual. I cringe when I hear it because it is not aligned with God's perspective of me. I am asked to renounce it, send it to the cross, etcetera. I've done it robotically to prevent condemnation, but I do not believe I am afflicted by a spirit of infirmity. My heart is only receiving negative rather than any of the good Jesus has in store for me.

It has been explained to me that people do not mean that my actual spirit, connected to the Holy Spirit, is broken when they pray in this way. That's fine. The prayer is still not in agreement with God's perspective. People may not intend to speak death, but just like in the book of Job, many speak without knowledge.[119]

Charismatic Christians do not know what these prayers communicate to the disability community. When we mix ignorance with a pursuit of supernatural power divorced from love, the combination can be lethal. As I write these words, I again see the beautiful faces of friends who do not know Jesus. It is for their sakes, and for the sake of the holy blood that purchased their lives in advance that I cannot soften my words.

My secular and noncharismatic Christian friends will feel violated if we pray in this manner. They will hear cursing and encounter humiliation. They will hear people shaming them because of how their bodies look. Worse, think of what these "prayers" sound like to a group of people who live in the shadow of a society that presumes the worst about them and sometimes prefers them dead. Even loosely associating disability with the demonic has undertones of criminalizing disability as justification for our removal. That has happened historically, and it can happen again.

The secular world, and most of the church, cannot tell the difference between devil-focused prayers and the belief that people with disabilities are full of evil. Instead of coming closer to Jesus because he loves and sees differently than the stigmatizing world, the disability community will flee the scene. This is not a matter of educating people with disabilities about what is meant when we pray from this mindset. It is a matter of whether we communicate the heart of God to people. It makes zero difference what people say they mean if they are not speaking in agreement with the Father.

To the parents reading, consider how your hearts would respond if people saw your children from the perspective of damage, spiritualized that perception, and repeatedly articulated this over them. My dad has never and would never pray such things over me because he knows me. Anyone charismatic who has spent even a modicum of time with me should be able to quickly recognize that there is no demon impacting my existence. Abba knows me also. Because it is such a common prayer, I've asked the Father if I have a spirit of infirmity. Without exception, he always says no.

"Then, why do people speak it over me so much?" I asked once.

Because they do not see what I see, he answered.

These prayers are based upon an intellectual assumption that physical brokenness equals spiritual brokenness because it is visible and has lasted over time. An intellectual assumption is not the same as supernatural discernment, and it is unwise to equate the two. If we think there is a spirit of infirmity, we should check ourselves to see if it is based only upon our perception of external differences. If so, we cannot call such thoughts supernatural discernment. *Infirmity* is a complicated word for *weakness*. It does not require the supernatural wisdom or power of God to recognize that I have weakness in my body. The presence of the weakness does not mean I, or those like me, are afflicted by a spiritual force of darkness. Such discernment is not revelatory, does not exalt Jesus when applied thoughtlessly, and is only limitedly biblical.

LOOKING TO JESUS

Jesus's healing power is creative, holistic, and full of a Father-centered focus. In his ministry, Jesus does not source physical limitations to demonic oppression every time. The man born blind in John 9 was just that—born blind. Jesus does not cast a spirit of blindness or infirmity out of this man. He makes some mud with his spit and re-creates the man's eyes.[120] This is an allusion to Genesis 2:7 when God made Adam from the dust. It is a beautiful creative miracle.

A passage from which to draw biblical evidence for the connection between healing and deliverance is in Acts 10 where Peter describes his eyewitness testimony of Jesus's ministry to Cornelius and his family. Peter says,

> God anointed Jesus of Nazareth with the Holy Spirit and with power. He went about *doing good and healing all who were oppressed by the devil, for God was with him.* (Acts 10:38 ESV, emphasis added)

Many people read this verse as "Jesus did good *by* healing those oppressed by the devil" as if there is no *and* in the sentence. The *and* is translated from the Greek word *kai* with similar meaning and use here to its English equivalent.[121] Unless there is deeper nuance implied in the original text beyond the apparent sentence syntax, I see Peter describing two activities.

Let's take the Greek a little deeper. In the above verse, Luke records Peter describing Jesus's ministry with the verb εὐεργετῶν (*euergeton*) translated as *doing good*.[122] Earlier, in Acts 4:9, Peter describes his own actions with a similar word. When he is interrogated by the Sanhedrin after he and John extend Jesus's healing power to the man at the temple, Peter calls this healing a "good deed" (Acts 4:9 ESV). In the Greek, it's the noun εὐεργεσίᾳ (*euergesia*).[123] I'm no Greek scholar, but *euergeton* and *euergesia* are cognates—noun and verb forms of the same root word. In Acts 10:38 then, "doing good" equals miracle healings while "healing all who were oppressed by the devil" (ESV) is a description of deliverance. Peter witnessed both facets of Jesus's power. He is not saying everyone Jesus healed received demonic deliverance.

Deliverance is sometimes necessary to resolve physical conditions, like when Jesus delivers a woman in Luke:

> Now He was teaching in one of the synagogues on the Sabbath. And behold, there was a woman who had a spirit of infirmity eighteen years, and was bent over and could in no way raise herself up. But when Jesus saw her, He called her to Him and said to her, "Woman, you are loosed from your infirmity." And He laid His hands on her, and immediately she was made straight, and glorified God. (Luke 13:10–13 NKJV)

Jesus did not rebuke the spirit off this lady. He did not ask her to renounce anything. He did not shout at her. He simply told her she was free and touched her. The NIV translates Luke 13:12 as Jesus saying, "Woman, you are set free from your infirmity." For all those who have commanded a spirit of infirmity out of me, no one has ever gently touched me and said anything close to what Jesus told this woman.

The text of the passage clarifies that this woman was unable to move because of an oppressive spirit. This is scripturally differentiated from people disabled since birth or for a specific amount of time, likely through injury or the effects of illness.[124] There is no guessing; it is clear. Jesus could immediately tell that the woman in Luke 13 needed deliverance. It should not be difficult for people of the light to recognize actual spiritual darkness. But let's not be so focused on the devil that we forget to do anyone any good.

A 4:1 RATIO

There are sixteen unique incidents of healing in the Gospels[125] where the cause of the disability or sickness is not demonic (fifteen if you want to exclude the re-creation of the high priest servant's ear that Peter disassembled[126]—hard to call that "condition" a disability or sickness). In Acts, there are four specified healings[127]—three people with paralysis and one man with a fever and dysentery, none of which involved demonic deliverance.

In contrast, there are only five distinct incidents in the Gospels, and none in Acts, where the text specifically connects physical limitation to demonic forces. These include the above Luke passage plus a boy oppressed with a deaf-mute, seizure-causing spirit whom Jesus delivers after the transfiguration,[128] and two more instances in Matthew where a demon prevented someone from being able to see or speak.[129] Last, there is a brief record in Luke of Jesus delivering a man unable to speak due to a demonic spirit.[130]

Don't conclude that deafness, blindness, and the inability to speak are demonic by default. There is a man in Mark who is deaf and unable to speak. Jesus heals him without demonic deliverance.[131] Similarly, Mark records a healing of a man with blindness at Bethsaida, and there is likewise no deliverance necessary for this healing.[132] If you have been doing the math with me, there is nearly a four-to-one ratio of specific healings without spiritual deliverance in the New Testament alone.

Looking at the summary statements of supernatural activity in the Gospels and Acts, there is a distinction between acts of healing versus deliverance in all but one case, and they are never functionally equivalent in any of these texts.[133] The only time we find a summary statement where there is no distinction is when deliverance is left out of the picture altogether,[134] which does nothing to strengthen the claim that the Bible considers healing and deliverance to be the same. Rather, the Bible supports a separation between the two in most of its miracle references.

NATURAL PROBLEMS

Sin originated with the devil, so technically, the devil caused creation's brokenness indirectly through sin. When John explains that "the reason the Son of God appeared was to destroy the devil's work," he is referring to sin and its effects (1 John 3:8). The preceding sentence in verse 8 is "The one who does what is sinful is of the devil, because the devil has been sinning from the beginning." We'd have to remove this verse from its context and read extra meaning into it if we wanted to claim it implies that disability is demonic. It is more accurate to say that Satan is responsible for starting the deception, and Adam and Eve are responsible for opening the door to creation's decay through sin.

A biblical explanation of *disability* is found in Romans—disability exists because sin exists on a cosmic scale. Sin produced a world in which there is natural loss, as Paul illustrates:

> For the creation waits in eager expectation for the children of God to be revealed. For the creation was subjected to frustration, not by its own choice, but by the will of the one who subjected it, in hope that the creation itself will be liberated from its bondage to decay and brought into the freedom and glory of the children of God.
>
> We know that the whole creation has been groaning as in the pains of childbirth right up to the present time. Not only so, but we ourselves, who have the firstfruits of the Spirit, groan inwardly as we wait eagerly for our adoption to sonship, the redemption of our bodies. (Rom. 8:19–23)

Creation endures empty futility, and it will continue to endure some of it until Jesus restores all things. Jesus accomplished this restoration on the cross, and he and gave us authority to call that restoration forth in his name at any time. But there is still groaning, and some of our bodies groan louder than others.

I have a broken nervous system caused by the depletion of oxygen in my brain at birth. People with blindness cannot see. These are natural problems. Nobody would rebuke a spirit of infirmity off somebody with a broken arm. We would ask the Father to regrow the bone in Jesus's name. How are eyes and nerve cells any different?

There are times when it is appropriate to rebuke sickness. Jesus rebukes a fever when he heals Simon's mother-in-law in Luke.[135] But we should hesitate to use this example as an ultimatum for rebuking conditions in healing ministry. People with disabilities are not sick. Cerebral palsy is different from the flu. I do not need something to leave my body; there is nothing present that can leave. I need the healing touch of God to enter my body and restore its deficit. Our emphases matter.

WHILE IT IS YET DAY

I have happy news for both the Spirit-filled church and the disability community. Jesus is not concerned about diagnosing the spiritual cause of disability. It is not necessary for his healing power. He is also not focused on Satan. Jesus disarmed Satan's power long ago. Jesus is focused on representing the Father and bringing the Father's kingdom into the world.

John 9 provides an excellent corrective to a hyperfocus on the cause of disability:

> As he went along, he saw a man blind from birth. His disciples asked him, "Rabbi, who sinned, this man or his parents, that he was born blind?"
>
> "Neither this man nor his parents sinned," said Jesus, "but this happened so that the works of God might be displayed in him. As long as it is day, we must do the works of him who sent me. Night is coming, when no one can work. While I am in the world, I am the light of the world." (John 9:1–5)

Look closely at how Jesus resets his disciples' attention. Jesus says to keep working while it is day and reminds them that "While I am in the world, I am the light of the world" (John 9:5). The redirection is to follow Jesus as the Light and not distract ourselves trying to find the answer to all the world's pain. We must obey the Lord's redirection, keeping our eyes on the true Light of the World, and follow him while it is yet day.

Returning to the Eric Gilmour teaching referenced earlier, he reminds us,

> He [Jesus] is like a giant magnet. Everything about Him pulls everything about you to Himself. When

you see Christ rightly, you can't but be pulled towards Him. That's why it's important as we preach the Gospel to show Him in His beauty and His love. Because when they see Him rightly, He pulls them towards Him. That He would die for them when they don't deserve it. That He would love them enough—this is the key to drawing people to Christ.[136]

As ambassadors for God's kingdom, everything we do should point back to the beautiful gospel of undefiled access. Rather than elevating performance over love and praying from sin or Satan-conscious mindsets, our prayers can reinforce the love and beauty of God. What would it be like for people to pray that my nervous system would encounter the Father's affection? Such a prayer exalts God's majestically good heart.

All healing ministries should orient us toward a God who desires us to be with him. This desire is so strong that Jesus died to satisfy it. As we pursue the hearts of people with God's love and confirm it with his power, we can use everything we have been given to live the gospel. Even our gathering spaces can become object lessons of the loving access we have to God in Jesus.

CHAPTER 11

Love Makes a Way

Access Is Love, a popular disability advocacy group, "aims to help build a world in which accessibility is understood as an act of love."¹³⁷ The creators of this organization are close to the gospel. God is love, and his love provides access in the Son. As the cross teaches us, accessibility is an act of love. Love makes a way for people to come close.

In his prayer before the cross, Jesus shares the primary motivation behind his choice to obey the Father at great cost. He prays, "Father, I want those you have given me to be with me where I am, and to see my glory, the glory you have given me because you loved me before the creation of the world" (John 17:24). Jesus died for us because he wanted us with him forever. He wanted his glorious presence to be eternally accessible to us.

As I introduced in chapter 1, accessibility communicates a

desire for a relationship to people with disabilities. Inaccessibility signals rejection. In making our gathering spaces accessible, Christians tangibly express the love of God. The prioritization of accessibility allows believers to offer a practical taste of the perfect, undefiled access we have to the Father through Jesus.

THE BUILDING WITH NO STRIVING

The Whole Person, a nonprofit in Kansas City, is built according to Universal Design standards. Ireland's Centre for Excellence in Universal Design describes the concept as "the design and composition of an environment so that it can be accessed, understood and used to the greatest extent possible by all people regardless of their age, size, ability or disability."[138] This maximal access for all is undergirded by the value that "if an environment is accessible, usable, convenient and a pleasure to use, everyone benefits."[139] The overarching goal of Universal Design is to move the accessibility conversation away from accommodating differences and toward creating spaces where the access is intentionally and proactively embedded into a structure from the outset.

The Whole Person took my breath away. I found an earthly building that represents the biblical idea of rest from human striving. Rather than having one accessible door with an automatic button, the front doors were hands-free sliding doors like the ones in a large grocery store. A ramp, not stairs, was the primary point of entry. Everything—from the wall colors to the hallway width, flooring, and acoustics—was intentionally crafted for as many people as possible to use with ease. In a video on the Whole Person's website, the architect explains,

> Every thought for this building was intended to be about how do we let the building speak to the users that come in and have them understand that this is a special place that is actually not so special that it can't be done anywhere else. That it really is intended to create a built environment that is very welcoming for others, and for all, and that no matter who you are, it will work for you.[140]

The intentionality reminded me of God's heart. While none of us know what God is designing for those who love him in eternity,[141] each facet of the new heaven and earth will be overflowing with joyful intentionality. Jesus has been long preparing this place for us. It will be accessible, restful, and an absolute pleasure in every exquisite detail.

ARGUMENTS AGAINST ACCESSIBILITY

Conversations about the accessibility of Christian gathering spaces can be charged with emotion. I will not be angling this discussion toward condemnation, nor attempting to set an unrealistic standard. If a church has the resources and the heart to include Universal Design principles in its next renovation, go for it. I do not have this expectation though.

The disability community does not want accessible perfection. We understand the difficulty of accounting for such a vast range of human needs. We are brilliant adapters and can make almost anything work—almost anything. All we ask is for you to help us get a little closer to good access so we can all more freely enjoy the Lord together. Please meet us halfway in the accessibility dialogue.

As gently as possible, I will answer the arguments I have heard against accessibility in the church over the years. Some of these perspectives come from a genuine place. They just misapply the biblical value structure involved. I want to reset the value structure so we can align ourselves with what is important over what is inconsequent.

No One Is Asking for It
It is common to hear, "Nobody is asking for access, so we won't consider providing anything extra until someone asks." This mindset can also sound like, "I don't see any disabled people in my church. If somebody comes, we will think about accommodations."

There is a fine line between proactivity and retroactive responsiveness to church accessibility. On the one hand, leaders with no disability experience, personally or professionally, may not have enough accessibility knowledge to be able to incorporate access into service structures and event planning. Understandably then, it becomes the responsibility of the disability community to educate on best access practices and inform the leadership of existing barriers. None of us expect the able-bodied world to be able to read our minds about what we need.

On the other hand, it is possible to set an access baseline without the prerequisite of specified expertise and to communicate the desire to make Christian spaces accessible. Communication of this desire is critical. If the heart for access exists, the disability community will help churches accomplish that goal in mutually beneficial ways. If the value for accessibility is not communicated, we generally stay away from the topic or remove ourselves from those spaces.

Just because people with disabilities may not often be in our gatherings, that does not mean they do not want to come or would not attend if churches prioritized access. Inaccessibility communicates we are not wanted, and no one remains in places where they feel unwanted or must struggle to participate. Because most disabled people still struggle for access across all dimensions of life, there is often a cap on the energy we can expend on advocacy in the church.

I will use the example of an American Sign Language (ASL) interpreter to illustrate the relationship between proactivity and responding to identified needs. The Deaf do not expect there to be a sign language interpreter automatically everywhere they go. This is not realistic. Instead, if they want to attend an event, the Deaf look for communication in event promotional materials (e.g., websites, social media, print sources) where they can make access requests in advance so that an interpreter can be arranged. A good practice is a simple statement like "Requests for accessibility needs can be made to (name of staff person)" with multiple methods of contact listed. To people with disabilities, these statements function like flags that this church will do what it can to provide accessibility. Intentionality matters. More of the disability community will come to our gatherings if we demonstrate to them that we care about access.

Convenience for Many

The convenience-for-many argument sounds like "Just because they have a disability does not mean we can make our ministry all about them. We have to think about reaching as many people as possible." On the surface, this argument has an appearance of wisdom, and I agree with the overarching goal. God does not value disabled people above nondisabled people. He equally wants everyone to be saved and to enter his kingdom. I also want to reach as many people as possible with the gospel.

But this is a worldly argument, not a biblical one. Its underlying premise is that unless we prioritize convenience for many, the gospel will not prosper and the church will not grow. The fastest-growing church in the world is in Iran, which is hardly a location where it is convenient to be Christian.[142] Moreover, this mindset reveals how the value system is being set. The claim that the Western church needs to cater to people's convenience to be successful is based on the world's marketing strategies. If the goal is to run a successful program where we define success in terms of numbers, this argument makes sense. If the goal is to glorify Jesus and honor the gospel, it does not make sense.

God is not limited by what is convenient for many. God is the one who draws people to himself and makes them hungry to know him. If people are hungry, they will come at the cost of inconvenience. But God does not want people to be excluded from our gatherings because we did not make space. The rubber meets the road when we see that this mindset bars people with disabilities from the community of believers.

When access is not prioritized, the inconvenience scale is weighted heavily against the disability community. We can have a discussion about convenience and spiritual hunger when the church at large restricts water during the day so they do not have to go to the restroom in small groups at someone's inaccessible house. This is the price I repeatedly pay to access such settings. I am beyond thankful to anyone who has carried me upstairs to a house or an apartment where we met, but I am still sacrificing. If I am out of my wheelchair, I will not be going to the bathroom for the duration of the meeting. Even if I am in my wheelchair, I usually cannot fit into the restroom in other people's houses. For years, I was able to do this safely, but my body is weaker now and cannot always handle the strain.

Also, many people cannot be carried up the stairs for medical reasons. It is just not an option. The convenience argument crumbles because the disability community is often paying an excessive cost for God's corporate presence. When the inconvenience scale is so imbalanced, our bank account will eventually go into the red.

In college, I had unobstructed access to a small, corporate

gathering. I regularly attended a worship-and-prayer meeting held in one of the classrooms of our student center. I lived in a dorm connected to the student center. All I had to do was get in an elevator, go up to the third floor, and I was there. We met Mondays, Tuesdays, and Thursdays my freshman year, and I went to most groups. I was always sad when we canceled because I was so happy to be there. Everybody around me was impressed by my hunger. What nobody saw as soon as the elevator doors closed on the way up was my delighted, happy dance of joy because I had such easeful access. I am sure my face was radiant. For the first and only time, the goodness of God's heart we enjoyed together came truly without cost.

Interrupting the Preferred Aesthetics
We often prefer small gatherings because they are considered to be a more intimate setting. For the same reason, we tend to prioritize the aesthetics of a setting or building over accessibility. There is nothing wrong with wanting to offer the Lord a space of beauty. We were made to create beauty, and God deserves excellence. But excellence according to whose definition?

One Good Friday, I led a prayer gathering to remember the hours Jesus was on the cross. I wanted the room to be beautiful, and I am grateful to those who helped me set up the space. We turned the fluorescent lights off and used softer, muted lighting. I bought a long piece of purple velvet cloth to drape over one of the tables where I placed communion, Bibles, and a few devotional resources. I used artwork from my apartment to decorate.

But none of these elements made the room beautiful. It was beautiful because thirty people filled with the Spirit of God came to remember and love Jesus. Together, we represented the temple of the Lord, and he showed up to be among us and in us.

I planned times for reading the Scripture, and if a brother or sister with a visual or learning disability came and needed better lighting to read with us, the fluorescents would have been turned on in a flash. Lighting does not matter. God's presence is not connected to the earthly arrangements of space. God inhabits the praises of his people.[143] When we come together to worship, he is among us no matter what the setting looks like. Creating beautiful spaces is fine as long as the priority is set according to what is ultimately valuable.

It is joyful news that access to God's precious presence is not dependent upon our surroundings. It is not about sound, light, or physical comfort. If it was, there would have been no earthquake that shook the prison doors open as Paul and Silas sang to Jesus in their chains.[144] It would be hard to describe their situation as an intimate setting, but such it was to the Holy Spirit. May we learn from their example. May we ask God to train us how to seek him in discomfort. We must learn to do it now when the stakes are still low. As pressures increase in the world, we will then have history with the Lord's heart to strengthen us. I am not suggesting we intentionally put ourselves into physical pain. We just need to ask Jesus to unshackle us from the mindset that his presence is related to our preferences.

Prioritization of Resources

Access can cost money, and I understand every church has limited financial resources. It is difficult, though, to justify complaints that accessibility costs are too high if congregations spend large amounts of money on visual effects and ambient surroundings. If a church can afford state-of-the-art audio-visual systems, they can make proactive arrangements to have captioning for sermons and not fear the cost of ASL interpreters when they are requested.

With the amount of planning and money that goes into large-scale conferences, basic accessibility standards should be provided proactively (e.g., live and closed-captioning, ASL interpreters, electronic formats for written content, adequate seating for mobility-device users). With all the technology available in our time, there is no excuse not to put accessibility on the front burner of large-scale gatherings. If cost is a legitimate concern, ask the Father to provide. He values the disability community, and he will finance access. Include accessibility in the conference budget from the outset.

Speaking to the smaller congregations, do not automatically limit yourselves. Accessibility is not always expensive. Some of the best access I ever experienced was in a small church. Any disabled person coming to a small gathering is not going to expect large-scale accommodations. On the whole, we are sensitive and respectful. Most of us would be delighted and honored that someone simply asked how they could help. We also know more about available resources to control costs.

If leading a house church, ask the Father how to make the space as accessible as possible. Maybe it is possible to build a ramp or have a portable one on hand that is measured to fit the exterior staircase. If the stairs are too steep for any ramp, maybe consider moving to a different location. At a minimum, it is good to have a plan in place for a wheelchair or walker user to get inside.

Those two steps are important across all types of settings—pray and plan. The best type of planning meeting would include people with different types of disabilities. We can tell you what we need and strategize together about how to get there. Invite us in.

Last but not least, please do not argue against accessibility by saying, "We will just get everybody healed, and then we will not need it." This attitude is foolish at best and presumptive at worst. It divorces power from love. If our gatherings are accessible, people will be healed in more ways than one.

ACCESSIBILITY AS OBEDIENCE

In chapter 2, I said we are on shaky ground if we say that some commands from Jesus apply to us while others do not. In that vein, Luke 14 is not a suggestion. It is a command, a piece of authoritative instruction equal with, if not weightier than, his instructions to heal. Jesus says,

> When you give a luncheon or dinner, do not invite your friends, your brothers or sisters, your relatives, or your rich neighbors; if you do, they may invite

> you back and so you will be repaid. But when you give a banquet, invite the poor, the crippled, the lame, the blind, and you will be blessed. Although they cannot repay you, you will be repaid at the resurrection of the righteous. (Luke 14:12–14)

What banquet is he talking about? We can invite people with disabilities to have a meal with us, but Jesus is not only referring to lunch here. He instructs us to proactively invite the rejected of the world system into the kingdom of God. Jesus implies our gatherings should be accessible. He wants people with disabilities in the banquet hall, not stuck outside the door.

Jesus goes on to share a parable about a man who prepared a great banquet and invited his guests.[145] The first guests choose not to come because they are busy. So, the master tells his servant, "Go out quickly into the streets and alleys of the town and bring in the poor, the crippled, the blind and the lame" (Luke 14:21). The servant obeys, but there is still room for more people. This time, the master instructs a servant, "Go out to the roads and country lanes and compel them to come in, so that my house will be full" (Luke 14:23).

There are a couple of things to note in this passage:

1. The disability community is expressly invited. The point of the parable is to explain the heart behind the instructions given immediately before it.
2. The disability community comes.

The servant reports back to the master: "Sir, . . . what you ordered has been done, but there is still room" (Luke 14:22). The initial strategy worked; people with disabilities accepted the invite to the banquet and came through the door. The rejects of the world system often say yes to Jesus, the great remover of rejection.

Successful ministry necessitates following the Lord's instructions as given. In the book *Keeping the Fire*, missionary Rolland Baker beautifully describes this truth:

> We not only go low before God, we go low before others. We do this by choosing not to seek favor with those who are influential when we begin to cry out to God for revival in a city or a nation. We go first to those who have no voice and no food. We go to the poor, the destitute, the bruised, the sick, the widowed, the orphaned, the forgotten, the ostracized, the outcasts and the dying. We who behave as nobodies before God who go to those who are regarded as nobodies by man.[146]

In the Western church, it is easy to practice exceptionalism toward great men and women like Heidi and Rolland Baker because of the fruit in their lives. Yet, few of us seem willing to follow the same steps in our contexts. We want the glamour of revival and supernatural power without giving spiritual and physical dignity to the overlooked of the earth.

NO UTILITY ARGUMENTS

Caring for the overlooked does not mean that we turn people with disabilities into our pet projects. It is not about us doing good deeds for our self-satisfaction. No, we humble ourselves so that we can lift people into their identities in Jesus.

I do not like utility arguments offered as a means to obey Luke 14, but it seems like everyone else camps out there. Here are three ways people might finish the argument "Include disabled people in the church because..."

- Their brokenness will keep us humble (Beates's view).
- Their lives reflect the image of a disabled God (Kenny's view).
- They exist so we can demonstrate God's healing power (Charismatic view).

These perspectives communicate that only until people with disabilities become useful will they be worthy of an invitation. All such utility arguments miss the point of Luke 14. Jesus's command has nothing to do with how much the church receives back from disabled people. Jesus reinforces that "they cannot repay" (Luke 14:14). Why do Christians of all streams keep creating artificial repayment plans?

Jesus pursues the disability community for the same reasons he pursues everyone else. Jesus wants disabled people with him so they may see his glory. We are not pet projects to Jesus. We are not his object lessons. We are people he desires. If Christians need another reason to obediently include us in God's kingdom, then let's all repent. Jesus does promise his followers will be blessed if they obey this command. Obedience always leads to blessing.

Our culture is highly sensitive to concepts of justice and evidence of hypocrisy. Those outside the church measure how we treat people with disabilities as evidence of our faith or lack thereof. I once had to steer a personal assistant away from anger after I explained an accessibility problem in a church that was not addressed well. She had overheard another conversation and asked me about it. I gave her a factual answer, careful not to gossip against anyone.

Her sense of justice was violated. She asked me, "Is there anybody I can call?"

I laughed and said, "There is nobody to call, but Jesus always gets me where I need to go."

With the help of some friends, I was able to get around that barrier. But it was possible to remove the barrier altogether if the conversation had been allowed to continue, and that would have been far better. How much sweeter would it have been if my assistant could have seen an example of God's people tangibly making space for me and others?

Other faiths and spiritualities are happy to be accessible. These groups view accessibility as a matter of integrity and, ironically, a way to attract as many people as possible. If the church does not learn to partner with Jesus's heart for access, we will be on track to lose many people with disabilities and their nondisabled friends to the new age movement and other false spiritual practices.

ACCESSIBILITY BASICS

The Internet is a great starting point for accessibility information. There are free online accessibility guides for all types of events and settings. Almost every United States county is served by a Center for Independent Living (CIL), an organization that exists to provide free accessibility expertise to their communities. Most CILs maintain lists of local sign language interpreters and can provide information on how to set up closed- or real-time captioning. A staff member can also do an accessibility walk-through of any building and point out the structural barriers for people with disabilities. Joni and Friends is another robust interdenominational resource for churches that want to improve accessibility. I include information on Centers for Independent Living as well as Joni and Friends in the resource section at the end of the book.

Below I have listed common accessibility needs according to the type of disability. This list is by no means exhaustive. I cannot anticipate every access need any more than the able-bodied world, but these are the basics with some best-practice tips included.

Hard of Hearing/Deaf

- **Provide a channel for communication assistance requests.**

    When listing a staff person who coordinates access requests, provide multiple methods of contact (e.g., phone and email).

- **Create closed-captioning for all recorded video content.**

    Do not rely solely on platforms like YouTube for their video captioning. These are better than nothing but can be so low quality that the content is unintelligible. Try watching a favorite sermon with the sound turned off and the YouTube captions rolling to get a picture of what this is like for the Deaf. Write transcripts for video content and create unique captions. YouTube has the option to upload a captioning file with any video.

- **Create written transcripts for all pre-recorded audio-only content (e.g., sermon podcasts).**

    Transcripts can be quickly and easily created with transcription software. After a transcript is made, it can be posted on a website alongside video and audio content.

- **Offer qualified ASL interpreters at church gatherings who are available during the message, ministry time, and if possible, worship.**

    At a minimum, create a channel to request ASL interpreter services. Some interpreters may be willing to interpret pro bono for a church or other nonprofit. Survey your congregation and see if there is anyone who already knows sign language and would be interested in interpreting during services.

- **Set up Communication Access Real-Time Translation services (CART) for live events, especially conferences.**

    CART works similar to real-time language interpretation services. With CART, a transcript of spoken audio is produced live and projected on a screen or personal device. Technology is ever advancing, and there is affordable live-transcription software (e.g., Otter.ai).

Blind/Low Vision

- **Plan event locations close to public transportation or offer rideshare transportation to events.**

- **Keep primary exterior and interior pathways clear from obstruction (e.g., sound system cords, equipment, etc.).**

- **Avoid rapid changes in lighting.**

  Use normal indoor lighting during messages and transition times between services.

- **Provide electronic versions of message notes and announcement content.**

  Many people with low vision use magnifying capabilities on smartphones as an alternative to print media, so they appreciate links or QR codes to electronic flyers rather than paper flyers or handouts.

- **Maintain excellent website accessibility standards so that online content is viewable for low-vision users.**

  Web accessibility includes compatibility with magnification software and screen readers. Screen readers are software that reads online content aloud. The compatibility of a website with a screen reader is based on how it is coded (often via HTML headings and tags). Web access also involves clear, consistent site navigation and strong color contrast so that text is easy to read. Hire web designers who have web accessibility expertise for the creation and maintenance of websites.

Intellectual/Socio-Emotional Disabilities

- Vary content in messages—use videos in teaching and provide concrete examples of concepts and demonstrations.

- Produce curriculum content that caters to multiple learning styles—visual, kinesthetic (experiential learning), auditory, and reading-based content.

- Dedicate a quiet space for people to go if they become overstimulated during a service.

- Treat adults like adults. If redirecting behavior, maintain an attitude of humility and respect.

Physical/Mobility Disabilities

- Keep exterior/interior pathways clear from cords, equipment, etc.

- Dedicate accessible parking spaces.

- Create at least one accessible route of entry, preferably at or near the main entrance of a building.
  This means a ramp or stairless entry leading to an accessible door.

- **When possible, use seating with removable chairs, so seats can be flexibly arranged for anyone who comes.**

    Movie-theater style seating only offers places for one or two wheelchairs at a time, which limits how many mobility-device users can attend. Families with infants or young children also often need these spaces for strollers. The more available spaces, the better for all. Lecture-hall seating (with a stair on each level) also prevents people with mobility devices from being able to move around the space (e.g., come forward for prayer during ministry time).

- **When possible, have at least one unisex restroom in addition to accessible stalls in gender-specified restrooms.**

    Unisex restrooms are helpful for people who may need assistance in the restroom from an opposite-sex caregiver (e.g., husband assisting his wife, mother assisting her adult son).

- **Maintain access to small gatherings.**

    Reach out to wheelchair users in the congregation to see if they would be willing to host a small group. Their homes are accessible automatically. As an alternative to small groups in an apartment or house, host at least one weekly group at the main church building. These buildings are generally more accessible than private homes.

LOVE IS ACCESS

In closing this chapter, I want to reinforce the holistic value of access to the local body of the Messiah. Beyond its evangelistic witness, accessibility in the church matters because none of us can successfully live as Christians without each other. I will always believe I have access to the Father, but this access does not negate how much I need my brothers and sisters. Paul prays that the church in Ephesus "may have power, together with all the Lord's holy people, to grasp how wide and long and high and deep is the love of Christ, and to know this love that surpasses knowledge—that you may be filled to the measure of all the fullness of God" (Eph. 3:18–19). We can know a measure of God's love individually, but only together can we get anywhere close to fullness.

During the worst of the spiritual warfare I faced while writing this book, I hit a moment of crisis. I was in trouble, believing the accusations of the enemy against my relationship with the Lord. My body was also hurting everywhere. I had an infection. One Saturday evening, the Holy Spirit whispered to my heart, *Promise me that you will go get prayer tomorrow morning.*

I obediently came up for prayer during ministry time at the end of Sunday service. A woman who I had never met before approached me, and I briefly summarized the emotional and physical circumstances. This sister listened to the Holy Spirit, receiving several words of knowledge about the specifics of what had been happening. She spoke the truth of the Father over my life and heart, which began to dismantle the accuser's voice. She prayed for my physical needs too while staying connected to the Father's heart for me.

At one point, she paused and said, "If your quiet place with the Lord is the only place you get any relief, don't worry about staying there too long."

What a fountain of life these words were to me. When I could not always believe my own words at the time, I could believe her words. Two weeks after praying for me, she brought me three laminated papers with Scriptures on them for me to read, meditate on, and trust. These Scriptures are now taped to my bedroom wall where I can see them during the day. She gave me treasure. Truly, if this sister had not come to lift me up, I might still be brokenhearted.

What if the entrance to my church only had stairs?

What if I was deaf, and there was no one to interpret for me during prayer?

What if I was blind and could not find transportation to church?

What if I had social anxiety and would have preferred to raise my hand for someone to come to me during ministry, so I did not have to push through a throng of people?

Accessibility is critical because of how much we all need one another, especially as we see the pressures in the world increasing around us. We find confirmation of this truth in Hebrews.

> Let us hold unswervingly to the hope we profess, for he who promised is faithful. And let us consider how we may spur one another on toward love and

good deeds, not giving up meeting together, as some are in the habit of doing, but encouraging one another—and *all the more as you see the Day approaching*. (Heb. 10:23–25, emphasis added)

It is impossible to "to hold unswervingly" unless we have encouragement from fellow believers. Let's prioritize access for one another to one another. God's healing power is also best available when we are together. We turn next to Jesus-centered supernatural healing.

CHAPTER 12

Love Touches Deeply

I often wonder how nondisabled charismatics read the healing accounts in Jesus's ministry and acts. What aspects move your hearts? Is there distance between you and these healings? What do you see?

I could never approach them from the posture of a dispassionate observer. There is no distance for me. I do not read the healing accounts in the New Testament as "Jesus heals. The end." Nor do I read them and think, *Look at what Jesus does for those people*. All are personal, and I attend to the rich details of each.

For this chapter, I analyzed every record of healing in the Gospels and in Acts, cataloging them according to their major themes. I wanted to see what patterns emerged between these themes. I did not count records of demonic oppression because those are technically deliverances, not healings. I also did not count resurrections. Sorry, Lazarus.

There are a myriad of ways to categorize these narratives, and for my purposes, I examined the value principles involved for us to emulate in healing ministry. I cannot go through all of them in-depth, but I will touch on most of them. I also will not include some of the healings I've already discussed in previous chapters.

Get excited, though! Jesus is a magnificent healer. Grab a Bible and come along with me as we walk together down dusty first-century roads, following Jesus the Messiah.

THE GLOBAL AND THE SPECIFIC

Before we start down the path ahead, we need to give attention first to the scenery around us. Starting in Mark's gospel and continuing through Acts, there is a consistent fluctuation between summaries of mass healings and accounts of specific miracles. This dual emphasis is like playing with the Google Earth satellite. We zoom out to get a glimpse of our nation or the whole planet and then type in our addresses to see a shockingly specific image of our houses through the same technology. The New Testament is likewise interwoven with healing from specific and global perspectives.

In Mark's and Luke's gospels, Jesus's first healing is Simon's mother-in-law, which is immediately followed by a large gathering and many healings.[147] Next, we see two specific healings, a man with leprosy and a man with paralysis. Matthew introduces us to Jesus's healing power generally first[148] and then dives into the specifics. This dance between the global and personal perspectives on Jesus's healing ministry continues across the

Synoptic Gospels (Mark, Matthew, Luke), the Gospel of John, and Acts. Luke contains the most accounts of specific healings while Acts records the most healing summaries.

The juxtaposition of mass healings with specific encounters is not accidental. God's healing power can both occur at scale and deeply impact the individual. Minimizing either side of this coin to the other is problematic. The charismatic church tends to emphasize the global perspective to the loss of individualized restoration. I have heard arguments for levels of healing, sometimes referred to as *anointing levels* and *glory levels*. The *glory level* would be Peter's shadow or Paul's handkerchief touching sick people to heal them,[149] and Jesus touching a man with leprosy for healing would be the *anointing level*. The glory-level type of healing ministry is then elevated as the most desirable because it is power at scale.

I am undecided about the biblical accuracy of such levels. If they exist, I certainly cannot find a value hierarchy between them in the Scripture. I see one Anointed One, the Messiah, who gives the Holy Spirit to those who ask. The Holy Spirit works both individually and at scale, but mass healings do not have greater significance in God's kingdom. Moreover, even when he is working at scale, the Holy Spirit is still forever personal.

One of the gravest errors charismatic Christians can make when we talk about the manifest glory of God, the Holy Spirit, is to use language that separates his glory from his person. The Holy Spirit is a person. He is not a force. The glory resembling a cloud that dwelled in the tabernacle and the Jerusalem temple was his person. His glory and personhood are inseparable. As

I write, I feel the zeal of the Lord burning in my heart over this issue. I have zero interest in any power, tangible or not, that is disconnected from the triune personhood of God. Impersonal power should never be our aim.

The combination in the Scripture between global and specific healings indicates we should not become so enamored with grand power displays that we forget God's personal pursuit of the human heart. If God valued mass healings over loving the individual, we would not have all the specific healings, some intentionally repeated throughout the Gospels.

Although there is less of an emphasis in Acts on individual healings, we cannot carry over the assumption that the Holy Spirit values numbers above people. He is God, and in tandem with the Father and the Son, he chooses people every time. He is not insecure about his healing ministry, and he does not need numbers to justify its success. Rather, it is in the aggregation of specific power demonstrations through love that healing can occur at scale. Now that we have this background scenery in view, we are ready to take our first steps down Jesus's healing road.

THEME 1: GOD'S RELENTLESS PURSUIT OF THE HUMAN HEART

A Man with Leprosy

Jesus possesses a singular capability to nuclearize healing power deep into the hearts of people. Such is the case with a man Jesus heals from leprosy:

> A man with leprosy came and knelt in front of Jesus, begging to be healed. "If you are willing, you can heal me and make me clean," he said.
>
> Moved with compassion, Jesus reached out and touched him. "I am willing," he said. "Be healed!" Instantly the leprosy disappeared, and the man was healed. (Mark 1:40–42 NLT)

Touch was the absolute last thing anyone would have expected, especially the man needing healing. People with leprosy were required to isolate themselves from everyone to avoid the spread of the disease. When they did interact with people, they had to shout, "Unclean! Unclean!" wherever they went so that people would know to keep their distance.[150] If anyone touched someone with leprosy, they became unclean and could no longer participate in regular social and religious life until they were certified clean by a priest. We do not know how long this man had leprosy. Imagine what it would be like to not be touched for possibly years and to have people shun you wherever you went as if you were the disease itself.

Jesus breaks the bondage of this man's rejection and stigma with one movement while simultaneously restoring his physical skin. He deliberately pursues the healing of this man's heart and body at the same time. He could have just spoken a word, but he chose to heal with his own hand. The beauty of Jesus in this story overwhelms me. He did not have to heal the way that he did. Yet in doing so, Jesus reveals the heart of the Father—a creative, compassionate God whose healing love touches much deeper than the physical.

The Roof Guy

The holistic healing from leprosy is followed shortly in the Synoptics by another healing with a similar theme. A friend group brings a paralyzed man to Jesus. They interrupt Jesus's public teaching by lowering the guy through the roof on a mat into the house where Jesus is preaching. Matthew records Jesus's initial response to the man: "Take heart, son; your sins are forgiven" (Matt. 9:2). Upon hearing this, the religious leaders immediately think that Jesus committed blasphemy.

Jesus responds to them, saying,

> "Why do you entertain evil thoughts in your hearts? Which is easier: to say, 'Your sins are forgiven,' or to say, 'Get up and walk'? But I want you to know that the Son of Man has authority on earth to forgive sins." So he said to the paralyzed man, "Get up, take your mat and go home." Then the man got up and went home. When the crowd saw this, they were filled with awe; and they praised God, who had given such authority to man. (Matt. 9:4–8)

To see the breathtaking depth of this miracle, we need to consider the religious, cultural, and personal context. From the religious angle, Jesus blows the lid off the first-century canister.

First, he forgives this man's sin. Second, he calls himself the Son of Man, which is a reference to the Messiah from Daniel 7.

In the cultural landscape, disability was considered to be the product of personal or family sin. We know this from the question that Jesus's disciples ask about the man born blind in John.[151] To Jesus's audience, the cultural connection between sin and disability would have been automatic.

Against this religious and cultural background, the man was lowered into an extremely risky situation. Beyond the intensity of interrupting a rabbi's teaching, he is being lowered through the roof. As someone who cannot walk, I assure you the vulnerability level is likewise through the roof. He is paralyzed. He cannot move. He cannot leave the situation if he wanted to. We do not know for certain if he wanted to go through the roof or not. Scripture does not tell us. Those unable to walk are often in situations simply because their caregivers brought them there.

It is at least possible from the social-religious context that the last place this man desired to be was in front of another religious man who would use him as an example of sin's outcome for the benefit of the congregation. We can reasonably assume that is what the Pharisees would have done to someone in this man's position.

Because we know who Jesus is, we often project the end outcome when we read Scripture. The people in the Scripture, though, cannot see the outcome of their actions. He may have been excited to meet Jesus, but he could have also been very nervous.

Regardless, Jesus perceives the deeper need in this man's heart. He says, "Take heart, son; your sins are forgiven" (Matt. 9:2). You can feel the tension shift when Jesus speaks. Imagine the relief this man experienced as the weight of guilt and condemnation melted in a moment at Jesus's words. I bet he was stunned.

After the religious authorities are offended by the forgiveness, Jesus heals the guy to demonstrate his authority as the Son of Man to forgive sin. Jesus was certainly addressing the Pharisees here, but he was likewise cementing his authority over sin to the man he healed. It was, after all, this man's sin he forgave only seconds before.

Now the roof guy has no excuse except to believe he is forgiven. Every step he takes is a tangible, functional reminder.

Left foot . . . your sins are forgiven.

Right foot . . . your sins are forgiven.

Left foot . . . your sins are forgiven.

Right foot . . . your sins are forgiven.

He will ponder his forgiveness every day for the rest of his life because Jesus soldered the miraculous healing to his heart's deeper need for mercy.

When I discovered the powerful heart soldering in this miracle almost a decade ago, I was lost in wonder. The first person I told was my Southern Baptist friend, Jonathan. I went to his house for dinner, and we discussed the Scripture. I was like, "Bro, are you seeing what I'm seeing?" Jonathan saw what I saw, and we sat together in awe for a moment. I will forever live in wonder toward Jesus. He majestically does his Father's work and reveals through it both his own identity and what the Father is truly like. Years later, the potent goodness of this healing still makes my heart tremble.

The Man Born Blind

Of all the New Testament healings, it does not get much sweeter than John 9. I mentioned it briefly in chapter 10 to show how Jesus refocuses his disciple's attention away from cultural and religious assumptions about disability. The end of the story is yet another example of Jesus interweaving healing with the heart of a person. The act of healing itself in this case was not heart-connected. Jesus spits on the ground, makes mud, puts it on the man's eyes, and tells him to "wash in the Pool of Siloam" (John 9:7). The man obeys Jesus, and he is healed after cleaning the mud from his eyes.

This story seems quite strange if you do not know the biblical allusion referenced. Like God forming Adam from the dust at creation, Jesus re-creates this man's eyes from the mud. In this healing, John is subtly reinforcing the divinity of Jesus to his audience. This is one of the best examples in the Scripture of a creative miracle, demonstrating that Jesus was and continues to be involved in the creation and re-creation of the earth.

John leaves us little time to appreciate the symbolism, however. The tension escalates quickly. The religious leaders are offended Jesus made mud on the Sabbath and healed someone. They thoroughly question the healed man about the specifics of the miracle, involving his parents to verify their son was born blind. The parents avoid the responsibility of testifying to their son's healing because they are fearful of the religious leaders who were threatening to throw out of the synagogue anyone who believed in Jesus as the Messiah.[152]

The authorities call the healed man to stand before them again. After some back-and-forth about his testimony, the angered leaders exclaim, "You are this fellow's disciple! We are disciples of Moses! We know that God spoke to Moses, but as for this fellow, we don't even know where he comes from" (John 9:28–29).

The man replies with one of the best comebacks in the Bible:

> The man answered, "Now that is remarkable! You don't know where he comes from, yet he opened my eyes. We know that God does not listen to sinners. He listens to the godly person who does his will. Nobody has ever heard of opening the eyes of a man born blind. If this man were not from God, he could do nothing." (John 9:30–33)

His testimony to the truth does not go over well. The leaders respond, "'You were steeped in sin at birth; how dare you lecture us!' And they threw him out" (John 9:34).

Throwing a person out of the local synagogue does not merely mean he cannot attend worship services any longer. Although scholars debate the details of the practice in Jesus's day, it nevertheless indicates removal from the religious and social community.[153] High stakes indeed for his faithful testimony.

Notice the majesty of what Jesus does next:

> Jesus heard that they had thrown him out, and when he found him, he said, "Do you believe in the Son of Man?"
>
> "Who is he, sir?" the man asked. "Tell me so that I may believe in him."
>
> Jesus said, "You have now seen him; in fact, he is the one speaking with you." (John 9:35–37)

Jesus seeks the man out, and then connects the revelation of his identity as the Messiah to the healing miracle received—"you have seen him." The intentionality of this tender moment between the Lord and this faithful man ruins me. Jesus chose his words deliberately. He intended the connection between healing and revelation. I do not think it is contextually incorrect to paraphrase Jesus's answer to the Son of Man question as, "You can see me with your own eyes."

Another beautiful detail here is that by sharing his identity as the Messiah, Jesus invites the man into a new community to replace the one he just lost. Jesus did not explicitly tell everybody that he was the Messiah, but he told this man. Although the Scripture does not say, I speculate he could have been among the first 120 disciples who gathered after Jesus's resurrection and ascension. There was no going home for him. His testimony produced ostracizing persecution. Yet, Jesus invites him into a new fellowship of believers.

The magnitude of this invitation goes a touch deeper. This man was born blind, born into severe stigma. All his adult life at least, he lived on the fringes of society begging for alms to survive.[154] Jesus's invitation into his community was likely the first invitation into something that this man ever received. He accepts. The only proper response to Jesus at this juncture is, "Lord, I believe," followed by worship.[155]

THEME 2: JESUS PROTECTS THE VALUE OF PEOPLE ABOVE POWER

In almost all the healing accounts, Jesus shepherds people's value, prioritizing it above a mere demonstration of power. This theme functions like an umbrella under which the others seem to fit. The three healings discussed for the heart-pursuit theme also qualify as a protection of human value. I separated them so we could more easily see the nuances. While not every healing shows an immediate connection to the heart of the person healed, nearly all of them safeguard the worth of people.

The Sabbath healings in the Gospels demonstrate Jesus protecting the value of people over cultural and religious priorities. Before the mandate of Luke 14 to invite the disability community into God's kingdom, Jesus heals someone on the Sabbath while eating in the home of a Pharisee. Jesus asks the Pharisees and experts in the law who were there, "Is it lawful to heal on the Sabbath or not?" (Luke 14:3). They don't answer him, so he heals the man, and then asks, "If one of you has a child or an ox that falls into a well on the Sabbath day, will you not immediately pull it out?" (Luke 14:5). In nearly all the other Sabbath healings, we see a similar exchange between Jesus and the religious leaders of his day.[156] Jesus makes it clear that bringing restoration to the lives of people takes priority above strict adherence to tradition.

The Bleeding Woman
Let's return to the woman healed from bleeding. It serves as a bridge between themes one and two because it belongs in both categories. By elevating her value, Jesus also responds to a personal heart cry.

Similar to the man with leprosy, we have a conflict between purity laws and Jesus's healing ministry. This woman has been living with continuous menstrual bleeding for twelve years. As a result, she is unclean. She cannot participate in regular worship and must keep herself separated from people so that she will not make them unclean and prohibit their participation.[157] No wonder she had tried many doctors, even though she was only growing worse.

Enter Jesus of Nazareth, the healer whose fame was ever increasing in Galilee and the surrounding regions. I will let Luke tell the rest.

> As Jesus was on his way, the crowds almost crushed him. And a woman was there who had been subject

> to bleeding for twelve years, but no one could heal her. She came up behind him and touched the edge of his cloak, and immediately her bleeding stopped.
>
> "Who touched me?" Jesus asked.
>
> When they all denied it, Peter said, "Master, the people are crowding and pressing against you."
>
> But Jesus said, "Someone touched me; I know that power has gone out from me."
>
> Then the woman, seeing that she could not go unnoticed, came trembling and fell at his feet. In the presence of all the people, she told why she had touched him and how she had been instantly healed. Then he said to her, "Daughter, your faith has healed you. Go in peace." (Luke 8:42b–48)

The absolute last place this lady was supposed to be was in a dense crowd, and the absolute last thing she was supposed to do was touch a rabbi. She's trembling, terrified to confess what she had done. Add to that her awareness that Jesus is looking for her. He is not moving on until he finds her, and she knows she cannot remain unnoticed for long. Like the roof guy, she has maxed out the vulnerability meter.

When she approaches, Jesus is gentle toward her fear. Jesus reinforces her identity as a daughter, celebrates her faith, and then blesses her with peace. He shields her vulnerability and protects her value. Jesus actually defends her value even before he finds her.

Sandwiched between the healing and Jesus's comforting words, we see a Messiah who cared enough to turn around. If Jesus was motivated by demonstrations of healing power for their own sake, he would have never sought after the woman who touched him. He would have just kept walking. What's one more release of power to a man for whom power was anything but novel?

Most healing ministry applications of this story focus on the woman's pursuit of healing. While that dimension is important, it is only half of the equation. Mr. Pursuit turns around to meet her, and he will not stop looking until he finds her. Many people touched him for healing,[158] but she was the only person in Scripture who attempted to do it without being noticed. Because God is personal by nature, Jesus circumvented her plan. Power itself is never Jesus's goal, only a vehicle for restoring the created identity of the person before him.

Outside the Village

There are two unique healings in Mark's gospel that follow this pattern of protecting human value. Mark chronicles the healing of a man who was deaf and had a speech impediment.[159] After Jesus "took him aside, away from the crowd," Jesus heals him and commands that no one publicizes the miracle (Mark 7:33).

Mark shares a similar healing of someone who was blind at Bethsaida:

> They came to Bethsaida, and some people brought a blind man and begged Jesus to touch him. He took the blind man by the hand and led him outside the village. When he had spit on the man's eyes and put his hands on him, Jesus asked, "Do you see anything?"
>
> He looked up and said, "I see people; they look like trees walking around."
>
> Once more Jesus put his hands on the man's eyes. Then his eyes were opened, his sight was restored, and he saw everything clearly. Jesus sent him home, saying, "Don't even go into the village." (Mark 8:22–26)

A major theme in Mark is called the *messianic secret*, and both passages tie into that theme. The messianic secret is Jesus's tendency to not publicly reveal himself as the Messiah outside of prophetic references (e.g., Son of Man; Lord of the Sabbath) and the witness from the miracles themselves. This boundary was necessary because Jesus was not going to fulfill contemporary messianic expectations to overthrow Roman oppression. The messianic secret also meant that he was responsible for stewarding miracle power. Power is attractive, which is why Jesus often gave unobeyed instructions to limit the spreading of miracle testimonies as he finished his Father's work.

While I honor this highly visible dimension in Mark's gospel with the two healings described above, Jesus is also protecting the vulnerability of both men. Jesus does not make a show out of dramatic healing. He takes the deaf man privately aside and away from the crowd. Jesus likewise removes the blind man from the village before the healing and instructs him not to return. We find out from Matthew that Jesus did not have a favorable opinion toward Bethsaida,[160] and it could be that Jesus was protecting the man from the city's spiritual corruption.

Regardless of the specific reason, Jesus is showcasing that these men are not objects to be acted upon or to be used for aggrandizing the display of power. They are people fashioned in the image of God. God's healing power is not meant to function in any measure like a freak-show racket. Private healings may sometimes be the best way to demonstrate love to a person, especially someone with a significant disability. Although there is no reason to keep the messianic secret any longer, those receiving healing can share their testimonies after the fact. The healing itself does not have to be open to public scrutiny.

I have never heard a teaching on supernatural healing that highlights the significance of Jesus's actions here. Mark 8:22–26 is taught every day in seminars and schools of supernatural ministry. It is the text used to validate praying for healing more than once. Why is the appropriateness of private healing not likewise taught? Public power has its biblical merit. But I want the charismatic church to be a people who follow Jesus to the fullest measure and not neglect his less popular actions even if they happen without public fanfare.

WHAT ABOUT ACTS?

A shift occurs in the biblical story as Acts begins. Jesus ascends to heaven from the Mount of Olives, and ten days later, the Father and Jesus pour out the Holy Spirit on Jesus's 120 followers. These followers now have the Spirit of Jesus living inside them. That same day, Peter leads three thousand people to salvation in Jesus.

The healing dynamic shifts as well. Jesus is no longer physically on the earth, but his miracle power is still available through the Holy Spirit living in his followers. The purpose of the miraculous has not changed. Jesus's followers are empowered to do miracles to continue confirming Jesus as the Messiah.

Given the above, do the same themes in Jesus's healing ministry occur in Acts? Yes, to a degree. With only four specified healings in the entire book, there is a greater emphasis on general healing summaries. Of the specific healings mentioned, there are likewise fewer details provided (e.g., no purity laws broken, no mention of forgiveness, fewer descriptors of days, settings, and locations). Three men with paralysis are healed in Acts. The fourth healing is Publius's sick father-in-law, whom Paul heals while stranded on the island of Malta. Looking at the healing themes in Acts separately from the Gospels for a moment, its two most striking themes are:

1. Healings confirm the gospel, causing many to believe in Jesus.
2. Gospel-confirming healings result in persecution.

That said, Acts' most-detailed healing does carry over the Gospels' theme of lifting up people's value:

> One day Peter and John were going up to the temple at the time of prayer—at three in the afternoon. Now a man who was lame from birth was being carried to the temple gate called Beautiful, where he was put every day to beg from those going into the temple courts. When he saw Peter and John about to enter, he asked them for money. Peter looked straight at him, as did John. Then Peter said, "Look at us!" So the man gave them his attention, expecting to get something from them.
>
> Then Peter said, "Silver or gold I do not have, but what I do have I give you. In the name of Jesus Christ of Nazareth, walk." Taking him by the right hand, he helped him up, and instantly the man's feet and ankles became strong. He jumped to his feet and began to walk. Then he went with them into the temple courts, walking and jumping, and praising God. (Acts 3:1–8)

Based on the text, we know that this man has been used to being unseen all his life. He has been begging at the temple every day. He asks Peter and John for money without raising his eyes to them. He is accustomed to alms being tossed at him without any recognition of his personhood. Recognition of a person's value is not required to give alms.

But Peter and John have been well-trained to give differently. They see the person in front of them, and when he does not look back at them, Peter directs his gaze. Only upon eye contact and its person-to-person connection does Peter give what he has to this man. God's healing power is, and always will be, personal.

WHAT IS THE FATHER DOING?

What does all this mean for supernatural healing ministry in the charismatic church? How do we apply these principles?

I admit there is tension in advocating for individualized, personalized healing. This concept resists programmatic multiplication and is more difficult to systematically train. I understand that God is limitless in power. He responds to simple prayers like "be healed in the name of Jesus" in the same way that he answers prayers and actions that touch deeply into the hearts of people. I do not want to overcomplicate healing prayer, but our attempts to create prayer formulas have more to do with making prayer "easier" for charismatic Christians than authentically loving someone who needs healing. Fear shuts down creative love fast.

I once prayed for a man at a bus stop. He could barely walk, and I had to slow my chair to give him space to walk ahead of me. When we reached the bus stop, I introduced myself and asked him if he was in pain walking. He told me that both of his knees had no cartilage. The joints were bone on bone. I offered to pray for him, and he accepted. I do not remember the words of my prayer. It was short and simple. I had been nervous to pray for him, which made me rush what I was saying. I was not thinking about how best to love this man. I was thinking about how fast I could pray so I could get it over with and check the box in my head that at least I tried.

After we went our separate ways, I realized that I did not say the most obvious prayer. I forgot that he needed cartilage in his knees. I could have simply asked God to regrow the cartilage. Because I was only thinking about how to survive the few seconds of my awkward prayer, I missed the obvious. I also missed the chance to deeply see this man and, most important, to ask the Father what was on his heart for him. If I had taken the time to listen first, the Holy Spirit could have done much more in the few minutes available to him.

I do not condemn myself nor anyone else for neglecting to partner with God's heart for people when we pray. It is common. Our first order of business when we pray for healing, though, should always be to ask the Father what he is doing. Using our access to his heart and listening for his intentions and desires toward the one before us is not optional. It is the gold standard of healing ministry. Jesus was always looking and listening for what his Father was doing.

I have heard people scoff at the notion that Jesus waited for the Father's prompting or instructions before healing someone. I agree that he probably did not wait to be led before healing each person, but I would bet my life that Jesus remained in constant communication with the Father as he healed. After healing the disabled man at the pool of Bethesda, Jesus tells his ministry audience plainly,

> Very truly I tell you, the Son can do nothing by himself; he can do only what he sees his Father doing, because whatever the Father does the Son also does. For the Father loves the Son and shows him all he does. Yes, and he will show him even greater works than these, so that you will be amazed. (John 5:19–20)

I am amazed. Of course, Jesus listened to the Father. How else does he come up with touching a man to heal leprosy? How else does he both anticipate and validate the forgiveness the roof guy is longing for? Why else would he turn around to call one woman *Daughter* or move to protect the vulnerability of a blind man at Bethsaida? Why do Peter and John care enough to look a lifetime beggar in the eyes? Sons and daughters listen.

OPEN HEARTS

Jesus never stopped being God while he was on the earth. He was always omniscient and could have done all the miracles without listening to the Father. But Scripture shows us he chose to rely on his relationship with the Father and the power of the Holy Spirit in his earthly ministry. Moreover, the triune God has been working in tandem from eternity past, so we should not be surprised when we find Jesus listening to and obeying the Father. His disciples, having received the spirit of adoption, do the same. There are no easy ways to heal; there are no hard ways either. There are only healings that come from the love of the Father.

We are called to be people who listen closely and respond to what our Father wants to do through us on the earth. Obeying our Father's voice will require we abandon performance and formulas. We should expect supernatural ministry to be different more often than it forms patterns. Our Father is creative, and he will give the strategies of his loving, others-centric heart to sons and daughters who likewise have humble, open hearts.

CHAPTER 13

Love Restores Majestically

In March 2018, I saw a moving prophetic picture that occurred in real time. The word *vision* sounds intense, but I will use it for brevity's sake. I was awake, and it was like watching a movie, only I was also in the movie. I saw myself seated on a small mat on a grassy hillside among a crowd of people listening to Jesus teach. Jesus noticed me, and he stood and walked over to where I was. I cannot say what he looked like. Those details were unclear. I just knew it was him.

He knelt in front of me so we could look one another in the eye. He smiled, and we simply looked at one another for some minutes. I realized he could see the longing in my eyes to come closer to him. Without speaking to me, he put an arm around me, pulled me from my mat, and held me a few inches from his face—literally taking me to himself. We looked straight at each other without saying a word.

Then, I began to hear Jesus's dialogue with the Father. Jesus asked, *What do I do now?* He obeyed what he heard the Father answer, and I responded to Jesus's actions. The real Elizabeth responded. This question-obedience-response cycle occurred three times.

The details are so tender that I've yet to successfully read them aloud. When I get to this part of the vision as I read it, I stop making sound. The best summary is Jesus's declaration to the Father in John 17:26: "I have made you known to them, and will continue to make you known in order that the love you have for me may be in them and that I myself may be in them."

The third time Jesus asked his question, I heard the Father answer, *Take her with you.* So Jesus picked me up, put me on his back, and walked away from the crowd toward his disciples.

I initially questioned this part of the vision. I told Jesus, "You never asked me if I wanted to come with you. Doesn't that violate my free will? You can't just go picking people up."

The last time I offered this objection, he answered, *You heard the Father as well as I did,*[161] *and you didn't resist.*

No, I did not resist. I wanted to come, and in the vision, I had other questions. Jesus and his disciples started walking down the road. The disciples looked confused, but they did not say anything. I was still on Jesus's back, and I was also confused. Jesus had not healed me, and I was not exactly prime material for a cross-country mission trip. With these concerns churning inside, I lowered my head and whispered in Jesus's ear, "If you don't heal me, you and your people will have to take care of me."

It's my honor to care for you, Jesus replied, and he continued walking down the road.

The vision did not end there, but I promise to return to the ending. For now, we need to again consider the multiple ways God loves the disability community through his church. Healing is one, prophecy another, and care a critical third.

PRACTICAL LOVE

The most Jesus-like words anyone has ever said to me came from the lips of a coworker. It was March 2020 and COVID-19 was just beginning to impact our east-central Illinois community. I was in my coworker's office, telling her I had lost several personal assistants who would not be returning from spring break since the university campus was closing. Without missing a beat, she looked me square in the eyes and said, "If you are ever stuck in your bed and do not have a PA, you call me. I will come help you. I cannot tolerate the idea of you being stuck in your bed."

She did not know that the previous afternoon, I'd sobbed in the car as the weight of my care, an already heavy burden, had now become crushingly immense in the space of twenty-four hours. My mom had come to help as I navigated the initial crisis, but she would not be able to physically provide care for longer than a few days. My sister Rachel was making emergency backup plans for me to sleep on a mattress at her house in case the government blocked off interstate traffic, which would prevent my family from coming to help if needed. But it would still take seven hours for one of them to arrive in an emergency.

When I told Mom what my coworker told me, she replied, "See, God knows, and he is providing."

My coworker showed me practical love. She was willing to cover my vulnerability, just like Jesus. Her love meant more to me at that moment than hundreds of healing prayers. Not all disabled people need daily care, but for those of us who do, a willingness to meet those needs is often one of the best ways to love us. It is active love.

One of the best experiences in the Christian community that I've enjoyed to date was at a small charismatic church in Northwest Arkansas called The Pointe. I attended The Pointe during my undergraduate education. This tiny church welcomed me and embraced me as their sister in the Lord. They demonstrated tangible love by driving me to church every week, moving a chair from the front row so I had a place to sit, and even changing the oil in my van in the church parking lot. It may seem small, but routine car maintenance is extremely difficult when you cannot drive your car to the shop. Although we never saw the healing we prayed for, the kindness of this congregation left a permanent mark upon my life. None of them will lose their reward from Jesus for it. Access in this community was not perfect, but it was beautiful. I was free to simply be a daughter and sister in the Lord's house.

I recognize that this church could be more flexible toward my needs because they were small, and I do not expect every congregation to be the same. I attend a large church now, and in this setting, brothers and sisters also show up to care for me.

After I thanked a friend for carrying me in and out of a house for a worship-and-prayer gathering one evening, he replied, "I hope that someday I won't have to do that, but until then, I am glad to."

"Thank you for saying that," I answered, pondering the resonance between his words and Jesus's response to my concern in the vision.

Like how spouses need to hear "I love you" from each other alongside the acts of service they do for one another, statements like my friend's eliminate my internal guesswork. It is near impossible for me to assume my needs are not troublesome for those around me unless it is communicated occasionally. If I surveyed members of the disability community who require daily care, I'd find a high percentage of doubt and anxiety about people's response to our needs. We do not know people are truly okay with helping us unless they say so.

CONSISTENT EXPECTATIONS

I expect an increase in miracles wherever the gospel is going forth. I expect God to show up for and through his people. I have been prepared to ask Jesus to multiply food since I was a young girl, and I am always ready to agree with his heart for healing.

But there will be disability until the Lord returns. The creation will continue to groan until the sons and daughters of God are revealed in his glory at the end of the age. That is a biblical, metaphysical fact as sure as the final resurrection of the dead. The Spirit-filled church, then, needs to listen to the Father's heart for how to best care for the disability community. Biblical love goes beyond miracle power.

One topic I've not yet touched on is disability etiquette. This includes our words and common principles of respect toward people with disabilities.

Disability etiquette can be summarized into these four guidelines:

1. Talk to disabled people directly. This applies to ASL interpretation as well. If an interpreter is translating, maintain eye contact with the Deaf person. They are the ones speaking. The translator is merely facilitating.
2. Both *person with a disability* and *disabled person* are nonoffensive descriptors. If someone prefers a different term, they will tell you.
3. Avoid labeling situations in disability-related language (e.g., that's lame, retarded, etc.).
4. Choose humility if someone corrects your language.

Like accessibility, few in the disability community expect language perfection. I usually will not correct it because I prefer to spend my communicative energy elsewhere. I also have to correct my own word choice. The hardest speech pattern for me to unlearn is describing situations in disability language. This style of speaking is ingrained into American colloquial English, and most of us are not even aware of it. Whenever I think about this aspect of disability etiquette, I flash back to a lunch conversation with my friend Jonathan during which I described a situation as *lame*.

He looked at me with a confused expression and gently asked, "What did you say, Lizzie?"

After repeating the phrase, I realized the context of the word. Until that moment, it never occurred to me that *lame* might be a demeaning, derogatory descriptor. I had never thought deeply about it. I asked if he found that word offensive and apologized. In the next moment, we launched into a long, ongoing conversation about disability descriptions in Bible translations.

The NIV and NLT do the best jobs at translating the original languages into appropriate disability descriptors. One of the reasons I paraphrased some of the healing narratives, and switched translations at times, was to avoid negative descriptors that would be distracting for disabled readers who have little exposure to the texts. Even then, I could not avoid the language issues altogether. Please remember that seeing words in our Bible translations do not justify their use in speaking or preaching.

On that note, never make disability jokes when teaching from healing narratives. They are not funny. I heard a sermon joke once that was so hurtful, I could not believe it. The joke twisted a beautiful moment of Jesus restoring someone's body into a selfish gibe. While everyone else was laughing, I could hardly breathe. I quickly scanned the room and prayed an internal *thank you* that I was the only disabled person in my line of sight who heard it. There is no condemnation, but as those speaking in the Lord's name, this joking is out of place. In our speech, we are to be thoughtful and considerate.

MINISTRY ETIQUETTE

Disability etiquette applies to prayer and ministry time. When asking for permission to pray for someone, always speak to people with disabilities directly, not to whoever they may be with. The first thing I notice about anyone is whether they engage with me directly. Because people think I am not able to speak, they talk to my family or friends as if I was not there. If someone asks to pray for me in this manner, I automatically assume I am not truly seen, and all of my defenses engage against the potential for additional pain. Talk directly to disabled people. If they cannot respond, we will learn that quickly.

Do not probe for diagnosis information and medical history details. If someone approaches me to pray, I am seldom comfortable sharing diagnosis information because people will rebuke the diagnosis off or out of me. If I come forward for prayer, I am more likely to offer my diagnosis because, at that point, the information is given on my terms.

I experienced a healing prayer where these etiquette concerns happened simultaneously. A stranger approached my sister's car while we were sitting in a parking lot outside of a Christian ministry building. I was in the passenger seat, and Rebekah sat on the driver's side.

Rebekah rolled down the window, and the woman said, "I saw that your friend is in a wheelchair. What's the condition?"

Rebekah leaned back in her seat so I could see the woman and looked at me, waiting for my answer. Because the woman already assumed that I could not speak, the only thing I thought to do was answer her question. I gave her my diagnosis, and she prayed. I listened respectfully and received her prayer. She did rebuke my diagnosis, which I did not receive. She also told me that the Lord has heard all my prayers and will answer them. Her words comforted me, as she had no idea that the night before I'd prayed to the Father about healing. She prayed several times, and I sensed that she would not stop unless I stopped her. When there was a pause, I thanked her and kindly ended the conversation.

I wish I'd asked her to come to my side of the car before answering her diagnosis question. Then she would have not been praying across Rebekah. That would have also given me time to think about how I wanted to answer the diagnosis probe and overcome the momentary stress that she did not speak to me directly at first. I would have told her then, "I do not want to give you my diagnosis, but you can ask the Father what's on his heart for me, and I'll agree with you toward that." This is a much safer arrangement and allows me to maintain a voice in what is happening.

The one time I felt comfortable sharing diagnosis information with a stranger was, ironically, at a conference. A woman sat next to me, and we started a conversation. Instead of asking, "What's your problem?" or "Why are you in a wheelchair?" a few minutes into our dialogue, she asked me, "What do the doctors say you have?" I smiled in sincere delight that a diagnosis question could be framed in such tactful language without requiring me to compromise my belief that the diagnosis is separate from my being. I gladly told this woman what the doctors said I had, and we agreed together for healing.

I share these stories to remind us to be considerate when asking others to offer personal information during prayer. The name of a diagnosis is not necessary for God's healing power, and it is okay for people to decline sharing it. Ministry time is also not an appropriate setting to satisfy curiosities about disability. I sometimes end up sharing a truncated version of my life story before prayer because diagnosis questions lead to birth questions, which lead to family questions. I have a strong distaste for the question, "Do any of your sisters have *problems*?" How do I answer in a manner that respects myself and them?

Add to these questions rampant curiosity about why and how I live independently, and pretty soon, prayer has become a live Q&A on the lifestyle decision-making of Elizabeth Flora-Swick. I am happy to answer these questions once I have an authentic relationship with someone, but I do not want to share the details with strangers. A good etiquette principle is to not ask a disabled person questions during prayer we would not ask anyone else.

PLEASE STAND

It is common at the beginning of services and the end of teachings for a leader to invite everyone to stand for worship or ministry time. A simple, painless addition to this invitation communicates volumes of worth to people with disabilities, especially the physically disabled. Change the invitation to "please stand if you are able." Nondisabled people may think this phrasing would single out someone using a wheelchair or who otherwise cannot stand, but it actually accomplishes the opposite. It gives us space to exist.

I do not typically notice the invitation at the beginning of service, but I always notice it at the end of a teaching. When I am listening to a teaching, I forget I have a disability. I have an extremely low exhortation threshold, so by the conclusion of most messages, my thinking runs like this: *Yeah! Jesus is beautiful! Let's live the gospel and crush hell!*

"Everyone, please stand." The words hit me like I swallowed burning acid. The first opportunity to respond to the message is something I cannot do. I am instantly reminded of my difference, and I face an immediate choice. I can be offended and bitter, or I can yield my heart to the Lord and use my access.

As soon as I hear the invitation to stand, I feel the Holy Spirit's embrace and hear him whisper, *Don't drink the Kool-Aid, Elizabeth.* In translation, this means, "Don't yield to bitterness. I am here, and I have space for you." His words are enough, and I can circumvent the grief. However, I notice whenever a leader says, "If you're able, please stand." Then I do not have to think about the Kool-Aid.

Whenever I sit next to my dad at church, he does not stand at the closing invitation. Since I was a child, he either remained seated or picked me up to stand with him. It is not something we ever discussed. He just did it automatically. His action has been a tangible reminder of the Father's heart for me through the years. I learned that good fathers stay with their children until they are free. While I may not go to church with my dad much anymore, the Holy Spirit still sits with me. He stays where I am. We wait together, and while we wait, I hear him begin to sing.

THE SONG OF THE LORD

What song is the Holy Spirit singing? The Father's love song of delight over his redeemed sons and daughters. As Zephaniah prophesies,

> The Lord your God is with you,
>   the Mighty Warrior who saves.
> He will take great delight in you;
>   in his love he will no longer rebuke you,
>   but will rejoice over you with singing.
> (Zeph. 3:17)

His song is beautiful, strong, passionate, powerful, and sweet. It is the perfect harmony between gentle tenderness and overpowering delight somehow balanced with the rhythm of his affection. Once you hear it, you are never the same. The triune God knows this song very well, and together the Trinity takes such joy in directing it toward each of us. The song has unique notes arranged to intersect with and reclaim our hearts from the confusing clamor of the world's noise. While the rhythm is the same, the melody is specific and personal as it woos our hearts to respond and to join it.

Compatible with its uniqueness, the song of the Lord has one universal outcome. Shackles of stigma and shame cannot withstand the first note. They shatter. Here's that immediate outcome:

> I will remove from you
> > all who mourn over the loss of your
> appointed festivals,
> > which is a burden and reproach for you.
> At that time I will deal
> > with all who oppressed you.
> I will rescue the lame;
> > I will gather the exiles.
> I will give them praise and honor
> > in every land where they have suffered shame.
> > (Zeph. 3:18–19)

The first Zephaniah reference should be familiar to most Christians. The next two verses are less known. As a disabled

Christian, I know that prophetic promise quite well. The Messiah gathers the mournful and cancels oppression. He silences the stigma against people with disabilities and turns it into praise. He removes the world system's judgment against our value.

I was glad to see the TV show *The Chosen* incorporate Zephaniah 3:17–19 into their retelling of the healing at the pool of Bethesda. The show writers set the passage in the context of physical healing. In its most literal reading, the text emphasizes salvation and trading shame for dignity. But given the poetic language employed in biblical prophecy, I see an implied reversal of circumstances as well.

I suggest verse 17 should not be siloed from verses 18–19. Perhaps the Lord's song of delight over his sons and daughters is his tool of choice to restore their dignity and accomplish their healing. It would be just like him to set it up that way.

Growing up, I attended a summer camp for children with disabilities and their siblings called Camp Barnabas. In this space, our physical needs were met without struggle. We had phenomenal access everywhere. But the best part was a lullaby based on Zephaniah 3:17 that the leaders sang over us at the end of evening worship. I wish you all could have been there. At the first line, the affection of the Father would settle over the room, and everyone melted into peace. All the burdens of life with a disability disappeared. We were free to just be sons and daughters again. It was a sanctuary.

In these pages, my goal has been to demonstrate how the charismatic church can become a sanctuary for the disability community. We know how to communicate the invitation to bidirectional access in the gospel. We believe Jesus makes our spirits whole—a wholeness that exists despite any other limitations. Most important, we know how to hear the Father's heart for people and are well-equipped to join the song he is singing over their lives.

We can become a sanctuary, and we need to become it. People with disabilities are hungry. Invite them into the Lord's banqueting house where there is always plenty of bread and new wine. Oh yes, there is lots of warm, healing oil too.

OIL OF GLADNESS

As promised, I will take us back to the vision that opened this chapter—Jesus carrying me down a first-century road. In the vision, I realized that Jesus was walking straight toward Jerusalem, straight toward the cross with me on his back. Depending on whether you ask me or Jesus, you will get a slightly different reaction to what happened next. I was not prepared; he was ready.

The details are still too tender to share, but I saw Jesus healing me. The Holy Spirit cut the tape before I saw the outcome of Jesus's action though. He left me literally suspended in the moment, probably right where he wants me to stay. I did not originally interpret the ending as healing related. I considered the possibility, but I genuinely thought Jesus was being himself and pouring the Father's delight over me. He was drenching me in his oil of gladness,[162] and I could process little else. Jesus did not give me any warning. There was no "I'm healing you now" communication. For over two years, the ending remained an internal question mark.

When the Holy Spirit interpreted the ending in June 2020, the first words out of my mouth were, "Oh, Lord, don't mislead your servant![163] Why would you do it like *that*?"

I couldn't think of a sweeter way to do it, he answered.

Later that evening, I insisted, "You're going to have to confirm this on both sides of Scripture." After he confirmed it from multiple Old and New Testament examples[164], I yielded. "If it didn't drip with your nature, I wouldn't believe you," I said. "All right then, may it be to me according to your word."[165]

I have tested the vision and interpretation thoroughly:

1. No parts of it contradict Scripture or the gospel, and its value principles shine across both Testaments.
2. I shared the vision with someone and the main component of the interpretation with a few others.
3. The impact on my life indicates legitimacy.

I am stewarding the prophetic word to the best of my understanding and conscience. This chapter shares the parts I believe will strengthen the church at this moment in time. I am purposefully not giving the specifics because the specifics are not systematically reproducible. God did not disclose to me how he wants to heal all bodies for all time. He shared how he will heal *me*. God's pursuit and protection of a human heart are the transferable aspects.

After the Holy Spirit said he couldn't think of a sweeter way to heal me, I wept. His protection overwhelmed me most of all. God has decided to release his healing power in a setting where my heart would be deeply safe. I still have to open its tender places. But I am willing to keep my heart open because I can hear God's magnificent, triune heartbeat beckoning for my obedient response.

GOD'S *KALOS* HEART

A trustworthy validity test for prophetic encounters is if they produce grace, desire, and endurance to love God and others according to Jesus's example. A dual phenomenon occurs in my heart whenever I think of the vision. I experience revulsion toward sin and a longing for God to communicate his deep, tender love through my life to his world. I want to become like the love I tasted.

This desire stems from the consistency between the triune God who interacted with me in the vision and the character of God revealed in the Bible. The vision would not have value to me without this agreement. I experienced his power, goodness, forgiveness, joy, justice, love, mercy, and even his jealousy rushing at me in one moment.

There was also majesty involved—a majestic goodness I could never invent if I had a million lifetimes to do so. I encountered his compassion and delight fused together in a redemptive pursuit to heal me. The combination smashed my preconceived boxes of what healing could be like. But I would rather trust the majestic character of God at the cost of my boxes than maintain them for their own sake. Nearly five years after the vision, a part of me is still reeling from the impact of his heart touching mine.

The Greek word *kalos* in the Bible means *beautiful* and *good*.[166] In a dialogue about the vision and interpretation, I asked the Lord, "Why am I still so undone by this?"

Because it's good, he replied. *It's kalos.*

Chapter 8 opens with the pain of someone's healing prayer disconnected from the Father's heart. Jesus's touch that I witnessed represented the ultra-antithesis of that experience. My heart is still ruined by the vision because it revealed the depth to which God knows me and the sweetness of his redeeming friendship. The only one who would know to heal me like that would have to be the same person who formed me with his own hands. I encountered the Exodus God who used his love and power to reclaim my heart while, apparently, in the act of restoring my body.

NO FEAR IN LOVE

I must revise my statement in chapter 1 that the greatest miracle I've experienced was discovering my access to God's heart. The greatest miracle is how God shepherded my heart through the painful moments of healing-ministry-gone-wrong so I could look him in the eyes and respond to his healing love without fear. He invented me after all; he knows how to rewire me. He came through a door in my heart I never expected with an invitation so holy, good, and right, it shakes me to the core. I've accepted it, thrown all the pain into the fire of his delight, and watched the bitterness burn.

Imagine the shock I absorbed opening Keener's *Miracles Today* to Marlene's story—a healing testimony for our condition that included a vision about her healing. I had no shred of a clue that there was documented precedent.

I crumpled against my desk, exclaiming, "Oh, you so set me up for this!"

God shepherded Marlene into the understanding that healing was his plan for her. That's not the covenant journey I needed to travel with the Lord. I had lost the expectation of goodness in healing ministry. God had to reset my context so I could believe that he intended the experience of my healing to be as good as I knew his heart to be. Strategically placed between the vision and interpretation was my request for warm oil.[167] If he'd given me the interpretation prior to that conversation, I would've never believed him. God was so gracious to me.

Marlene and I would both agree a vision is not necessary to receive healing; Jesus has already made full provision. Nor would we claim some mystical secret or magic trick to God's healing power. We are two daughters living with undefiled access to the Father's heart for ourselves and for others.

Marlene's vision and my vision were different. She saw the specific church where the healing would happen and the date it would occur. I saw Jesus healing me in his first-century ministry, so there is a degree of metaphor in my case. The Holy Spirit's interpretation contained its own specificity, however, and I have no good reasons to doubt it. Marlene acted upon the Lord's word to her; I will do the same. Unlike Marlene, I cannot arrange the healing setting in the natural. All I can do is daily yield my heart to Jesus, which is just how he wants it.

When what he spoke of occurs, I will obey as Marlene did. I know exactly what I saw and exactly what I heard. So please do not pressure me against following God's word. I'm not open to changing course. God loves watching me believe him. He wants me to trust and proclaim his majestically good, *kalos* heart. He wants the same for you.

NO BETTER HOME

Some people may think I wrote this book merely to validate my expectations for healing. I gave much prayerful thought to whether I would include the vision because I did not want my motives to be misconstrued. I chose to add it in the final chapter because it bridges the healing content and the importance of care for the disability community. The vision touches both dimensions.

Its details form a chiasm.[168] The exchange originating from the Father's heart between Jesus and I at the beginning repeats at the end in reverse order. The turning point, the hinge, of the encounter is Jesus taking me with him and our brief conversation on the road. I understand how chiasms work; the turning point is vital.

It was through the safety Jesus provided in his recognition and acceptance of my need for care that fostered my capacity to receive what else he had for me. Healing or no healing, he was taking me with him. I could move on to the final part of the vision because I trusted him to cover my vulnerability. I felt protected. I was loved. The healing action itself flowed out of deep affection. When it happened, I was so lost in the goodness of his love, I did not recognize it.

It seemed dishonest to only share the first half of the vision and pretend the end did not connect to my healing. I never intended to downplay healing. I wanted us to see the wholehearted love of God for the disability community. The vision expressed his holy, beautiful love. I am not waiting for a prophetic word that agrees exactly with the vision before I let someone pray. I am waiting for love. I am waiting for the charismatic church to minister to people with disabilities from the triune God's majestic heartbeat. Shall we join the Lord in his song of delight?

Regarding my healing, I do not know when God will accomplish the specifics. But I'm along for this ride. Far off or near, I've seen enough of Jesus's glorious beauty and the greatness of the Father's heart to motivate me to share whatever good gifts he gives and extend the invitation to dwell in God's house all our days. I will be about my Father's business—to display his goodness in its depth and glory.

The Holy Spirit gave me the vision in my graduate school dorm room while I lived among disabled people. If anyone thinks I intend to be healed and waltz off into some sunset leaving the disability community in my dust, you have greatly underestimated the God who loves me. I am never going to stop sharing this love.

The way to the Father is open. When we live from the access Jesus gives us, the Holy Spirit enables us to display God's heart on the earth. We are free to dwell in the worldview house of our choosing. But I recommend the Trinity's house. There is no better home.

ADDITIONAL RESOURCES

To find your local Center for Independent Living (CIL) for guidance on accessibility in your community, see the Independent Living Research Utilization (ILRU) Directory: www.ilru.org/projects/cil-net/cil-center-and-association-directory

For information on accessibility and supports within churches and Christian ministries spaces, see the Joni & Friends Church Resources blog: www.joniandfriends.org/category/for-the-church

For more content from the author, see
www.elizabethfloraswick.com.

ACKNOWLEDGMENTS

My deepest gratitude to all who have helped bring this book to print. Thank you for your investment into the story God is writing with my life.

I want to specifically thank:

My parents—Mark and Jane Flora-Swick—for discipling me to hear the Holy Spirit's voice and base my life upon what he says.

My siblings (& in-laws)—Blake and Rachel Schulze, David and Hannah Dorton, Micah Flora-Swick, and Rebekah Flora-Swick—for your love, encouragement, and wisdom.

My nieces and nephews—Abigail, Judah, Isaiah, Hosanna, and Asher—for all the joy you bring to my heart.

John Swick "Grandpa"—for your listening ear and insights about publishing.

Evan and Emma Barber, Kyle Meythaler, John Chisolm, and Charlotte Russell—for reviewing the manuscript, providing feedback, and connecting me to resources.

Dianne Leman—for believing in this book and championing me throughout the publishing process.

Brian Blount—for writing a gracious, thoughtful foreword.

Endorsers—Chris Gore, Putty Putman, Mike Hutchings, Mike Bickle—for reading the manuscript and supporting my message.

Grace Lockett—for caring for me and enjoying my many theological ramblings.

Kassie Castaneda—for listening, believing me, and loving me with the Father's affection.

Janet Walsh—for lifting my gaze back to Jesus's face when I forgot where to look.

The Personal Assistants who worked for me during this writing journey—Chloë, Christine, Anna, Celeste, Zoe, Caitlyn, Jazmin, Natalie, Martyna, Myra, Jasmine, Hailey, Inna, Neka, Alex, Katy, Breanna, Kelsey, Marina, Emily, and Ava—for caring for me.

Thank you to all who gave toward publishing costs. I pray that the Lord blesses you a hundredfold for your generosity. My special thanks to:

Clay and Regina Harrington	Happy and Dianne Leman
Andrew and Sarah McIntyre	Karen Hoeffner-Grubbs
Brandon and Kelsey Barber	Meghan Scholtens
Rick and Karen Duggan	Nancy Giving
Tim and Joy King	Pat Dalton

NOTES

Introduction

1 ADA National Network, "What Is the Definition of Disability under the ADA?," ADA National Network: Information, Guidance, and Training on the Americans with Disabilities Act, last modified April 2022, https://adata.org/faq/what-definition-disability-under-ada.
2 Centers for Disease Control and Prevention (CDC), "CDC: 1 in 4 US Adults Live with a Disability" (August 16, 2018), https://www.cdc.gov/media/releases/2018/p0816-disability.html.
3 See John 14:17.
4 See John 14:26; Acts 13:26; 16:7; 20:22–23.

Chapter 1

5 See Gal. 5:16–18
6 See Hab. 2:14.
7 See 2 Cor. 5:6–7.
8 See 1 Pet. 1:8.
9 See Pss. 23:6; 27:4.
10 "You show that you are a letter from Christ, the result of our ministry, written not with ink but with the Spirit of the living God, not on tablets of stone but on tablets of human hearts" (2 Cor. 3:3).

11 See Col. 3:12.
12 See Rev. 4:1.
13 See Pss. 18:19; 2 Sam. 22:20.
14 See Phil. 3:20.
15 See Isa. 55:1–2.
16 See Heb. 10:19–23
17 See Rom. 5:6–21; 2 Cor. 5:21
18 See Rom. 6:11–14
19 Ccodyguy, "Why Do Only Some Get Healed?" (November 2, 2011), YouTube video, https://www.youtube.com/watch?v=0MOJBxaKWXo, 12:38–12:44.
20 Ccodyguy, "Why Do Only Some Get Healed?," 13:31–13:52.
21 See Rom. 11:17–18.
22 See John 1:36; Rev. 5:6–10.

Chapter 2

23 See Heb. 1:3; Col. 1:15.
24 See Rev. 21:1–5
25 See Matt. 10:1; Mark 6:7; Luke 9:1; 10:9.
26 See 1 Pet. 2:4.
27 See Mark 15; Matt 27; Luke 23; John 19.
28 See Col. 1:19–20.
29 See Mark 15:19.
30 Gallup, Inc., s.v. "context," Gallup CliftonStrengths, accessed January 23, 2022, https://www.gallup.com/cliftonstrengths/en/252209/context-theme.aspx.
31 See John 15:16.

Chapter 3

32 See Acts 3–4; 5:12–16; 6:8; 8:4–8; 9:32–35; 14:8–23.
33 See Acts 3:1–10; 9:32–35; 14:8–10. I'm not counting Paul's three-day blindness after his encounter with Jesus on the road to Damascus (See Acts 9:1–19). Although technically a healing,

the incident seems better categorized as God's temporary supernatural discipline rather than a healing of illness or naturally-caused disability.

34 See Acts 4:4.
35 See Acts 5:12–16; 6:8.
36 Craig S. Keener, *Miracles Today: The Supernatural Work of God in the Modern World* (Grand Rapids: Baker Academic, 2021), 35–36, Kindle.
37 See Acts 14:8–20.
38 See Luke 17:10.

Chapter 4

39 *Merriam-Webster*, s.v. "metaphysics," accessed January 23, 2022, https://www.merriam-webster.com/dictionary/metaphysics.
40 Kitty Cone, n.d., "Short History of the 504 Sit-in," Disability Rights Education & Defense Fund, accessed January 23, 2022, https://dredf.org/504-sit-in-20th-anniversary/short-history-of-the-504-sit-in.
41 Independent Living Research University (ILRU), "The Independent Living Movement: History and Philosophy to Implementation and Practice," (2011): 10, https://www.ilru.org/sites/default/files/resources/il_history/IL_Movement.pdf.
42 Emily Ladau, *Demystifying Disability: What to Know, What to Say, and How to Be an Ally* (California: Ten Speed Press, 2021), 30, Kindle.
43 Joseph P. Shapiro, *No Pity: People with Disabilities Forging a New Civil Rights Movement* (New York: Three Rivers Press, 1994), 12.
44 Shapiro, *No Pity*, 16.
45 Stella Young, "I'm Not Your Inspiration, Thank You Very Much," TEDxSydney (April 2014), https://www.ted.com/talks/stella_young_i_m_not_your_inspiration_thank_you_very_much?language=en.

Chapter 5

46 David Pfeiffer, "Eugenics and Disability Discrimination." *Disability & Society* 9, no. 4 (1994), accessed December 8, 2022, https://www.independentliving.org/docs1/pfeiffe1.html.
47 "Holocaust Memorial Day Trust | Disabled People," Holocaust Memorial Day Trust (2022), https://www.hmd.org.uk/learn-about-the-holocaust-and-genocides/nazi-persecution/disabled-people/.
48 Julian Quinones and Arijeta Lajka, "Why Down Syndrome in Iceland Has Almost Disappeared," CBS News (August 14, 2017), https://www.cbsnews.com/news/down-syndrome-iceland/.
49 Michelle Kaufman, "Eugenic Thought Is Alive and Well in New Zealand," Family Life International NZ (December 16, 2013), https://fli.org.nz/2013/12/17/eugenic-thought-is-alive-and-well-in-new-zealand/.
50 Joseph P. Shapiro, *No Pity: People with Disabilities Forging a New Civil Rights Movement* (New York: Three Rivers Press, 1994), 260.
51 National Council on Disability (NCD), "Genetic Testing and the Rush to Perfection: Part of the Bioethics and Disability Series" (October 23, 2019): 22, https://ncd.gov/sites/default/files/NCD_Genetic_Testing_Report_508.pdf.
52 Amy Kenny, *My Body Is Not a Prayer Request* (Grand Rapids: Baker Publishing Group, 2022), 1, Kindle.
53 www.elizabethfloraswick.com/blog.
54 Kenny, *My Body Is Not a Prayer Request*, 3.
55 Kenny, *My Body Is Not a Prayer Request*, 1.
56 Kenny, *My Body Is Not a Prayer Request*, 12.
57 Kenny, *My Body Is Not a Prayer Request*, 12–13.
58 "The man answered, 'Now that is remarkable! You don't know where he comes from, yet he opened my eyes. We know that God does not listen to sinners. He listens to the godly person who does his will. Nobody has ever heard of opening the eyes of a man born blind. If this man were not from God, he could do

nothing.' To this they replied, 'You were steeped in sin at birth; how dare you lecture us!' And they threw him out." John 9:30–34

59 Kenny, *My Body Is Not a Prayer Request*, 12–13.
60 Kenny, *My Body Is Not a Prayer Request*, 3.

Chapter 6

61 Craig S. Keener, *Miracles Today: The Supernatural Work of God in the Modern World* (Grand Rapids: Baker Academic, 2021), 110
62 Keener, *Miracles Today*, 110.
63 Keener, *Miracles Today*, 110–112.
64 Hamilton, *Exodus*, 42.
65 Hamilton, *Exodus*, 55.
66 See Ex. 5.
67 Hamilton, *Exodus*, 101.
68 Hamilton, *Exodus*, 103.
69 Hamilton, *Exodus*, 103.
70 See Ex. 7:1.
71 See Ex. 3:15–17; 4:29–30; 6:2–9.
72 See Ex. 9:15–16.
73 See Ex. 12:38.
74 Ladau, *Demystifying Disability*, 106.
75 See 2 Tim. 4:5.
76 See Deut. 8:3; Matt. 4:4.

Chapter 7

77 Watchman Nee, *The Spiritual Man, Reprinted as a Combined Edition* (New York: Christian Fellowship Publishers, Inc., 1977), 29–30.
78 See 1 Cor. 3:16; 6:19; Eph. 2:18–22.
79 See Eph. 1:7–10.
80 See Gal. 5:16–26; 6:7–10; 1 Pet. 1:22–23; 1 John 3:23–24.

81 See 1 Cor. 12:3.
82 Chris Gore and Angela Locke, *The Perfect Gift: Seeing the Child, Not the Condition* (self-pub., 2018), 38.
83 Gore and Locke, *The Perfect Gift*, 60–61.
84 Gore and Locke, *The Perfect Gift*, 17.
85 Gore and Locke, *The Perfect Gift*, 17.
86 Wayne Grudem, "What Is the Soul? Is It Different from the Spirit?," *Zondervan Academic* (blog, May 15, 2018), https://zondervanacademic.com/blog/what-is-the-soul.
87 Sean McDowell, "A Quest for the Historical Adam: A Conversation with William Lane Craig" (aired September 22, 2021), YouTube video, 34:07–35:00, 35:19–35:36, https://www.youtube.com/watch?v=8TQ8w_9qN4Q&t=2257s.
88 Sean McDowell, "A Quest for the Historical Adam: A Conversation with William Lane Craig" (aired September 22, 2021), YouTube video, 34:07–35:00, 35:19–35:36, https://www.youtube.com/watch?v=8TQ8w_9qN4Q&t=2257s.
89 See Rom. 12:2.
90 Devan Stahl and John F. Kilner, "The Image of God, Bioethics, and Persons with Profound Intellectual Disabilities," *Journal of the Christian Institute on Disability*, 6.1–6.2 (Spring/Summer & Fall/Winter 2017): 24, accessed January 23, 2022, https://journal.joniandfriends.org/index.php/jcid/article/view/143/33.
91 Stahl and Kilner, "The Image of God, Bioethics, and Persons with Profound Intellectual Disabilities," 24.
92 Michael S. Beates, *Disability and the Gospel: How God Uses Our Brokenness to Display His Grace* (Wheaton: Crossway, 2012), 131, Kindle.
93 Beates, *Disability and the Gospel*, 128.
94 Beates, *Disability and the Gospel*, 129.
95 Beates, *Disability and the Gospel*, 133.
96 See James 4:10.
97 Beates, *Disability and the Gospel*, 133.
98 C. S. Lewis, "The Weight of Glory and Other Addresses" (New York: William Collins, 2001), 45.

Chapter 8

99   Kathleen Stassen Berger, *The Developing Person: Through Childhood and Adolescence*, 9th ed. (New York: Worth Publishers, 2009), 374–375.
100 The Remnant Radio, "What Does Todd White Teach? Remnant Radio's Interview with Todd White (Part 3)" (aired December 9, 2020), YouTube video, 49:10–51:38, https://www.youtube.com/watch?v=6ZYnjec6aWk.
101 www.elizabethfloraswick.com/blog.

Chapter 9

102 See Acts 2:43; 4:29–31; 5:12; 14:3; 15:12.
103 See John 13:35.
104 See 1 John 4:7.
105 Ccodyguy, "Why Do Only Some Get Healed?, YouTube video, 14:51–15:34, https://www.youtube.com/watch?v=0MOJBxaKWXo.
106 Luke 4:13.
107 See Mark 2:1–12; Matt. 9:1–8; Luke 5:17–26; John 5:1–14.
108 See John 15:24.
109 See Mark 1:25; 9:25; Luke 4:35.
110 See John 11:43.
111 Mark 5:41.
112 See Acts 3–4:3.
113 See Acts 14:10.
114 Deut. 4:24.
115 See 2 Kings 5:1–14.

Chapter 10

116 See Rom. 11:17–18.
117 Eric Gilmour, "Beauty of the King || 50 Minute Teaching || Eric Gilmour" (aired February 7, 2021), YouTube video, 36:58–37:02, https://www.youtube.com/watch?v=7dpFHwhAwQo.

118 See 1 Pet. 1:22–23.
119 See Job 38:2.
120 See John 9:6
121 *Bible Hub*, s.v. "Acts 10:38," https://biblehub.com/interlinear/acts/10-38.htm, "Καὶ." https://biblehub.com/greek/kai_2532.htm.
122 *Bible Hub*, s.v. "Acts 10:38," https://biblehub.com/interlinear/acts/10-38.htm.
123 *Bible Hub*, s.v. "Acts 4:9," https://biblehub.com/interlinear/acts/4-9.htm.
124 See John 5:5; Acts 3:2; 9:33; 14:8.
125 See Mark 1:30–31; 1:40–45; 2:1–12; 3:1–6; 5:24–34; 7:31–37; 8:22–26; 10:46–52; Matt. 8:5–13; 9:27–31; Luke 14:1–6; 17:11–19; 22:50–51; John 4:46–54; John 5:1–9; 9:1–7. Cross references across the Synoptic Gospels are not listed.
126 See Luke 22:50–51.
127 See Acts 3:1–10; 9:32–35; 14:8–10; 28:8. As in chapter 3, I'm not including Paul's blindness in Acts 9:1–19. See also note 36.
128 See Mark 9:14–29; 3:7–10; 6:1–6; 6:12–13; 6:53–56; Matt. 17:14–21; 13:53–58; 14:34–36; 11:1–6; Luke 9:37–43; 9:6; 7:18–35 as examples.
129 See Matt. 9:32–34; 12:22.
130 See Luke 11:14.
131 See Mark 7:31–37.
132 See Mark 8:22–26.
133 See Mark 1:32–34; Luke 4:40–41; Matt. 3:24–25 as examples.
134 See Matt. 15:29–31.
135 See Luke 4:39.
136 Eric Gilmour, "Beauty of the King," 36:23–36:58.

Chapter 11

137 Alice Wong, "Access Is Love," Disability Visibility Project (February 1, 2019), https://disabilityvisibilityproject.com/2019/02/01/access-is-love/.

138 "What Is Universal Design," Centre for Excellence in Universal Design (National Disability Authority, n.d.), accessed January 24, 2022, https://universaldesign.ie/what-is-universal-design/.

139 "What Is Universal Design," https://universaldesign.ie/what-is-universal-design/.

140 The Whole Person, "3710 Main Street and Universal Design: The Story behind TWP's Headquarters," *The Whole Person*, accessed January 24, 2022, 1:55–2:15, https://thewholeperson.org/about/our-building.html.

141 See 1 Cor. 2:9.

142 "Day 2: The Fastest-Growing Church in the World," The Gospel Coalition (April 7, 2021), https://www.thegospelcoalition.org/article/fastest-growing-church-world/.

143 See Pss. 22:3.

144 See Acts 16:24–26.

145 See Luke 14:15–24 for the whole parable.

146 Rolland Baker, *Keeping the Fire—Sustaining Revival through Love: The Five Core Values of Iris Global* (United Kingdom: River Publishing, 2015), 71–72.

Chapter 12

147 See Mark 1:29–34; Luke 4:38–41.

148 See Matt. 3:23–25.

149 See Acts 5:12–16; 9:11–12.

150 See Lev. 13:45–46.

151 See John 9:2.

152 See John 9:13–23.

153 Craig S. Keener, *The Gospel of John: A Commentary* (Grand Rapids: Baker Academic), 787, 793, Kindle.

154 See John 9:8.

155 See John 9:38.

156 See Mark 3:1–6; Matt. 12:9–14; Luke 6:6–11; John 5:16–17.

157 See Lev. 15:19–32.

158 See Mark 6:53–56; Matt. 14:34–36.

159 See Mark 7:31–37.
160 See Matt. 11:21–22.

Chapter 13

161 See John 6:44–45.
162 See Isa. 61:3.
163 See 2 Kings 4:16.
164 I only included two of these confirmations in this book—the man with leprosy Jesus heals and the man Jesus forgives before healing his paralysis. While I intended the parallel imagery of a first century road in chapter 12 and chapter 13, I analyzed the NT healings for chapter 12 independent of confirming the vision.
165 See Luke 1:38 ESV.
166 *Bible Hub*, s.v. "2570 *kalós*," accessed May 2, 2022, https://biblehub.com/greek/2570.htm.
167 Timeline: the vision in March 2018, the warm oil conversation in September 2019, and the vision's interpretation in June 2020.
168 A *chiasm* is a literary structure in which parallel elements repeat after the middle element in reverse order to create a bracketing effect for emphasis.

Made in the USA
Coppell, TX
26 February 2023